The *La Ina* BOOK OF

TAPAS

Classic small dishes from Spain

Elisabeth Luard

MARTIN BOOKS

The author
Elisabeth Luard is a highly respected author whose fifteen-year
sojourn in Spain has provided the expertise and inspiration for this
book. She is acknowledged as having a specialisation in European
food styles, and with the publication of her book European Peasant
Cookery to universal acclaim, she has won a place in the highest
echelons of cookery writers.

Published by Martin Books
Simon & Schuster Consumer
Group
Grafton House
64 Maids Causeway
Cambridge
CB5 8DD

In association with
Domecq UK Ltd and
Eurobrands Ltd
45 New Street
Henley-on-Thames
Oxfordshire
RG9 2BP

First published 1989
Fourth impression 1995

Illustrations © Martin Books 1989
Text © Elisabeth Luard 1989, 1991
Second impression 1991
First impression photographs © Dent & Reuss Ltd 1989
Second impression photographs © Eurobrands Ltd 1991
Illustrations © Woodhead-Faulkner (Publishers) Ltd 1989, 1991

ISBN 0 85941 599 6 (hardback)
    0 85941 603 8 (paperback)

Recipe notes
All recipes give ingredients in metric, imperial and cup measures.
Use any one set of measurements, but not a mixture, in any one
recipe.
All spoon measures are given in level spoons, unless otherwise
stated. 1 tablespoon = one 15 ml spoon; 1 teaspoon = one 5 ml
spoon.
Eggs are standard (size 2–3), unless otherwise stated.
Wine and water measures are given in glass sizes. 1 small glass = ¼
sherry glass; 1 wine glass = approximately 150 ml (¼ pint) (⅔ cup);
1 large glass = 1 tumbler.
Fresh herbs are used, unless otherwise stated. Dried herbs can be
substituted for fresh, but halve the quantities.
Use freshly ground black pepper and coarse salt for salt and pepper.

Design: Andrew Shoolbred
Photography: Laurie Evans
Food preparation for photography: Berit Vinegrad
Styling for photography: Lesley Richardson
Illustrations: Helen Herbert
Typesetting: Pentacor Ltd, High Wycombe, Bucks
Printed and bound by BPC Wheatons Ltd, Exeter

Contents

Introduction

The food

Tapas are those delicious little titbits which are served as the accompaniment to a glass of wine in the bars of Spain – particularly those of Andalucía, whose native nectar is the clean, straw-pale fino sherry of Jerez. Until very recently, the price of the glass always included a tiny dish of the house speciality. Nowadays it is more likely that the tapas will be priced and served in full or half portions – on one plate, but with a fork for each participant. But the tapa itself – a 'lid' for the glass it accompanies – is traditionally no more than a mouthful.

'Que tiene de tapas?' – 'What is there to pick at?' – is the question every bartender expects. He will answer with a rhythmic, almost singing litany. He can repeat it, too, if asked – word for word, rhyme for rhyme.

Tapas embody a way of life: southern Spain lives outdoors, and in the long light summers, day and night merge into each other. With the heat of the sun, the bountiful Mediterranean, the fertile valleys and the white-washed villages under a perfect blue sky, the native Spaniard has a head-start on the road to happiness.

Spain's sunny south is the spiritual home of what is a *way* of eating, more than the eating itself. In Andalucía, the rhythm of life is gentle. Here the midday meal is habitually taken around two or three, and the evening meal not until ten or later. This leaves a long gap unbridged by the comforts of elevenses or tea-time. Tapas not only bridge the gap – the habit of going to bars for a glass of wine, and having a nibble of this and a taste of that, suits the Spanish temperament.

The Spaniard is naturally friendly and loves company, sitting out on the street of an evening and exchanging news and nods with passers-by. The tapa habit is a reflection of this delightful companionability. The practice allows the freedom to wander, to lean an elbow on the bar, chat to acquaintances, settle down at a table under the awning and keep an eye on the children. And the tiny dishes of food which accompany the wine keep the wanderer convivial and amiable. As *Don Quixote* was to the novel – picaresque, progressing in short bursts of self-contained drama – so tapas are to a conventional meal.

The *romerías* – local religious pilgrimages which turn into all-day picnics – reflect the country's delight in getting out and about and taking the air on high days and holidays. The ritual of the tapa bar – *tasca* or *chozo* or whatever it happens to be in the area – seems to be an extension of this pleasure. The tapa habit is essentially a wander from bar to bar, in search of special dishes and entertainment. The television rumbles on in one corner, like a kind of electronic Ancient Mariner. No one listens: the live theatre of the bar is far more interesting. In the old days an old sea-dog or villager would have performed a similar function to the 'telly', reciting yarns long since unheard. Nowadays he's been replaced by a politician on his platform, or a celebrity peddling dog food.

It was not until I went to live, with my husband and four young children, in a remote Andalucían valley, that I really learnt to appreciate the pleasures of this thoroughly Spanish arrangement. It is a natural way of life. The Spanish are visually articulate – Goya, Velázquez, El Greco, Picasso all testify to this passion. It's the *look* of the thing that Spain enjoys most, and the tapa bar puts its goods right out on display.

Our house was in the hills on the southernmost point of Europe, half-way between Algeciras, a busy seaport, and Tarifa, a small fortified harbour town which, locals assured us, had once been a Phoenician stronghold. The whole of Andalucía had been colonised by the Moors for five centuries, and their influence on the region remains strongly in evidence. This is apparent not least in Andaluz eating habits: Moorish spicing, almond sweetmeats, and a wide repertoire of rice dishes bear witness to their presence.

Once the children were settled in local schools, we began to look around for local entertainment. In the early seventies, there were no theatres nearer than Malaga. The red light district of Algeciras was the only area where good flamenco could be found, and that was not really family viewing! Films were poorly dubbed, cinema accommodation primitive, and television in its squalling infancy.

Feria – Spain's local carnivals – brought circuses and dancing to Algeciras in June, and to Tarifa in September. For the rest of the year, we instituted the regular Saturday family tapa 'hunt'.

With four children under ten (plus the odd visiting friend), we were perfectly in tune with local custom. In public places in Spain, children tumble underfoot everywhere. Babies accompany their parents, either curled into a Moses basket in the corner of the bar or slumbering on a maternal shoulder. Children are still the great prize, the reason for being, of the people of the Mediterranean. Grown-ups simply pay their way and hold their liquor. So all outings are family outings – perhaps not so much in the big cities, where life is a little less leisurely and business must at least be seen to be done – but certainly in the sun-warmed towns and villages of the south.

Sleepy schoolchildren slumber on benches while the adults gossip and flirt and argue. From an early age children have a splash of wine diluted with plenty of carbonated sweetened water (cream soda or fizzy lemonade) to qualify them for a little tapa along with the grown-ups. The atmosphere is leisurely – browsing and grazing are not exactly urgent occupations – and conversation is the only necessary accompaniment to a tapa. That and the pale sherry of Jerez – or even the good red wine of the fertile Ebro valley where Rioja is lovingly made by, among others, the same Domecq family – whatever you please. But there's no doubt that the dry pale sherries of Jerez go wonderfully well with certain dishes. Particularly those, when, as they say in Cádiz, the very sea-spray has been dipped in batter and fried in the olive oil of Sevilla. (Or Toledo; or Ronda; or wherever you feel the rich green juice of the Mediterranean's oldest cultivated fruit is at its best.)

Since we did not live in a village, we would make our way to our chosen locale and do the rounds. The nearest settlement, Pelayo, was famous for its bakery, and the roadside bar there served big chunks of bread with tiny bowls of snails in paprika sauce. The secondary bar – tucked away behind, and always full of old men playing draughts – had wonderful wild rabbit cooked with garlic. So that made a fine enough evening.

If we turned west down the road towards the Atlantic we could have spider crabs and sea snails in a bar set into the Moorish battlements of Tarifa, and then go on further, to the *chozo* down by the beach at Punta Paloma, for deep-fried quail and the fattest, crispest french fries in Spain.

Algeciras, on the Mediterranean side, offered the more sophisticated delicacies of a busy seaport. Down by the harbour was a bar which served big pink prawns as firm as lobster, baby cuttlefish fried to perfection, and clams and razor shells opened briefly on a scalding hotplate and served with quartered lemons. And in the deserted market place someone would have set up a brazier to blister juicy octopus tentacles over the hot coals. Unlike most of the locals, we usually found we could not manage to tuck into a large meal afterwards – a shortcoming which had something to do with our English habit of still taking tea and this-and-that throughout the day.

In a simple bar in a small village, the tapa offered with your glass of wine will be correspondingly modest. Perhaps a few home-cured green olives, a bit of local goat's cheese, or a cube of that thick potato omelette – Spanish tortilla – that any Spanish housewife seems to be able to turn out to perfection.

Big cities and towns – Barcelona, Seville, Malaga, Granada, Madrid – reflect in their bars and restaurants the affluence of their citizens. Customers progress from venue to venue, proud of their knowledge of house specialities, like truffle hounds scenting out the treasure.

Raw materials are very important in the cooking of Spain, as with all uncomplicated cuisines. Whether this is good bread and chorizo sausage, the freshest of shellfish, or a way of leaching and flavouring the best and plumpest of olives, each bar, *chozo* and *tasca* will have its own specialities. These may simply be the best salt-dried mountain ham – perhaps a black-skinned haunch from Jabugo; or a well-matured cheese – maybe a fine Manchego or a leaf-wrapped Cabrales. Alternatively, the house fame might rest on a little scalding casserole of *anguilas* – baby eels bathed in olive oil and spiked with chilli – or even some small delicacy which reflects the skill of the cook with the frying pan (skillet). No one fries better than a Spaniard, and among Spaniards, none better than the Andaluz.

Kitchen equipment dictates as firmly as ingredients. The *plancha* – a flat metal griddle heated underneath by a gas jet or charcoal – is used to grill (broil) sardines, prawns, thin slices of tuna or swordfish, and pork fillet marinated with garlic and paprika. In Seville I have seen a heavy old smoothing iron smacked on top of a chop to speed up the cooking process. In the hills behind Cordoba there is a bar which serves only quail's eggs fried on the *plancha*, dished up on a piece of bread cut to scale. Others rely on the little shallow earthenware casseroles which miraculously do not crack on direct heat: all cooks have their own special ways of making them fireproof (I rub them with garlic, fill them with water and leave them in a hot oven until the water boils dry). These casseroles are used to prepare many dishes, like shrimps in garlic and oil, self-saucing *kokochas* (hake throats), and wild mushrooms; even plain ham and eggs becomes a new pleasure. The most primitive tool of all is the brazier – a long metal tin filled with red-hot charcoal – over which fez-hatted travelling pedlars grill Moorish-spiced kebabs in the street during *feria*.

The drink

The classic drink of Andalucía, the perfect partner to a tapa, and in all probability the reason for the tradition itself, is fino sherry. Ask for a glass of wine in an Andaluz bar, and the odds are you will be poured a chilled glass of the dry, aromatic golden wine, whose flavour and bouquet is like no other.

Jerez has been producing wine for around three thousand years. Climate and geological conditions, an ancient expertise and the special solera system of ageing the wines, combine to make the wines of Jerez unique. The sherry-producing district is a triangular area bounded by two rivers – the Guadalquivir and the Guadalete – and the Atlantic ocean. The vineyards, set on rolling hills striped with well-pruned vines, in winter reveal a remarkably wide palette of soil in hues ranging from deep dark red to shimmering white. Soil colour is dictated by chalk content. The palest, *albariza*, is the chalkiest. *Albariza* nurtures the vines which produce the best sherry of all – the lovely dry pale finos, such as Domecq's Fino La Ina. Heavy, iron-rich *barro* (mud) has a higher yield, but produces coarser, heavier wines. The *arenas* (sandy soils) are good for sweet wine grapes, such as Pedro Ximenez. All are important in the production of Jerez's fine wines and brandies.

Proximity to the crowded sea-lanes of the Straits of Gibraltar has ensured that the town has played host to many visitors – some more welcome than others. The Phoenicians, Greeks, Carthaginians, Visigoths and Romans, all in their time pitched camp among the rolling hills. In AD 711 the Moors arrived; five centuries later they were still there. Five hundred years of Muslim rule left its imprint on the daily life of the people – from architecture to literature, popular music to culinary habit. During these five centuries, although alcohol was forbidden by the Koran, the vines were tended so that the grapes could be dried into raisins (a popular ingredient in Middle Eastern cookery). Nevertheless, wine continued to be made by the Christian inhabitants. When Jerez was recaptured from the Moors by Alfonso the Wise in 1264, the town became known as Jerez de la Frontera, as it then marked the frontier between Christian and Muslim Spain.

Jerez shipped its wines out of the port of Cádiz, whose busy quays were ideally placed to service the merchant ships plying between the Atlantic and the Mediterranean. British thirst for this 'sunshine-in-a-cask' has been dated back to the twelfth century. This was further enhanced by Sir Francis Drake who, raiding Cádiz in 1587, made off with the Armada's cellarful of sherris-sack (all 2,900 butts of it!) This involuntary bit of export did Jerez's trade more good than harm, since the British merrily took to the brew when their hero flooded the market on his return home. They have been re-ordering (usually rather less aggressively) ever since.

It is because of these repeat-orders that the wineries of Jerez are liberally sprinkled with English-sounding names. It was inevitable that the merchants and importers who became Jerez's most enthusiastic customers should entangle themselves both financially and matrimonially with the sherry-producing families. Nowadays these international connections remain as strong as ever.

The 250-year-old Jerez-based firm of Pedro Domecq, producers of Fino La Ina, has benefited from just such cross-fertilisation. The bodega was founded in 1730 by an Irishman, Patrick Murphy, who bought and worked vineyards below the town. On his death, a lifelong friend, a Jerez-based Frenchman named Haurie, took over the business in the absence of heirs. When Napoleon invaded Spain in 1808, Haurie's nephew, Jean Charles Haurie, was in charge. Haurie supported the French and was granted the apparently lucrative concession to supply wine to Napoleon's army. In the end, Haurie was never paid, and when the French were driven out, he barely escaped being killed as a collaborator.

The business was suddenly on the verge of ruin. It was saved only by the arrival from England of Pierre de Domecq, son of the first

Monsieur Haurie's sister, Catherine Haurie, who had married into an old aristocratic French family, the Domecqs of Béarn in the Basses-Pyrénées. The family had been obliged to flee across the Channel after 1789 to escape the Revolution's guillotine, and English-educated Pierre had been busy building a successful English agency for the family firm at the time of the disaster in Jerez. So in 1816 Pierre took control of the ailing Spanish end of the operation, changing his first name from Pierre to Pedro. In 1822 the company became officially known as Pedro Domecq. By the middle of the century the company had expanded to account for one-seventh of the whole sherry trade, with one thousand customers in England, and two thousand acres of land under viticulture.

Pedro died a millionaire at the early age of fifty-seven, leaving the business in the capable hands of younger brother Juan. For the next thirty years, Juan expanded the business, and having no heir, brought in his nephew, Pedro Domecq Loustau, to carry on the tradition. Loustau introduced Spain's first brandy to the company's range. Domecq had always distilled their own spirits for fortifying their sherries and had built a thriving trade by shipping the surplus production to Holland where it was used in liquor making. After a firm in Amsterdam had cancelled a large order for these spirits, it was discovered that after a few years left lying around in its barrels in a warehouse, the raw spirit had matured into a fine brandy. This founded a new tradition – brandy de Jerez – and it was consequently named Fundador (founder). Today the distiller's art is epitomised in Carlos I, known colloquially as 'Charlie', which takes twelve years to come through a solera, making it unique to Jerez.

Today the firm remains family-led, with a pride in horsemanship a close second to wine-making in the family interest. José Ignacio Domecq 'senior', known throughout the trade as 'The Nose' and a noted polo player in his time, still takes a great interest in the firm, now that his son José Ignacio Domecq 'junior' is personally responsible for blending and overseeing the entire range of Domecq wines. The range is led by La Ina, a pale straw-coloured wine with a hint of green – light, dry and delicate with a faint bouquet of almonds. Like all sherry it is at its best drunk within a few days of opening. For this reason it is widely available in half bottles in Spain – a trend which is gradually spreading to Britain. Fino is also best served well-chilled in the slender, narrow-topped sherry glasses known as *copitas*.

Fino La Ina is made from the Palomino grape, harvested in September. The grapes are crushed (in the old days, by men wearing hob-nailed boots), and the juice known as must is extracted.

Fermentation takes place in the bodega. These tall, airy buildings, high and shadowy as cathedrals, are built facing the Atlantic so that the ocean breezes can add their character to the wines.

By early spring, fermentation has left a wine that is completely dry. The wines are then drawn off to *añadas* – casks containing wines of one year only – and left to develop. This is the moment of truth for the wine, because during this time the cask may or may not develop the *flor* (Spanish for flower) – the film of yeast which covers the surface of the wine, and which only occurs in Jerez and a few other select areas of the world. In adjacent casks containing the wine of grapes from the same vineyard, one may produce flor and the other not. The flor is the magic ingredient in the pale dry finos.

This young fino wine is then aged in the solera system. Basically, a solera comprises of rows of barrels, usually stacked one on top of the other and graduated in age. From time to time a proportion of the younger wines are drawn down into the next oldest and more mature row. This process ensures that the perfectly mature fino graduates into the bottle at one end of the solera, while the younger wines gradually and patiently move up through the education system until they too are mature enough to graduate. There is no shortcut. These wines cannot be ascribed a vintage, since the solera system is a way of blending wines of different ages, and some soleras may be over a century old. All bodegas are proud of the ancient butts which contribute to their own particular, priceless, solera system. Domecq has a 259-year-old butt – 'Napoleon' – which is now so dark and concentrated as to be undrinkable neat, but (as demonstrated to fortunate visitors) the flavour of a single drop in a glass of La Ina is a revelation.

Amontillados are fino wines in which the flor has died or been killed by fortification with alcohol, and which have been left to acquire an amber colour and nutty dry flavour with age. Domecq's Primero and 51–1A are classic examples of this. The latter is the product of a solera founded in 1830 and is, therefore, on average sixty years old. The name is derived from the fifty-one barrels that go to make up the *criadera* or first layer of this solera.

Manzanillas are finos from the seaside town of Sanlúcar de Barrameda. Naturally crisp, dry and aromatic with a slightly salty tang, they can acquire fino characteristics by being aged in the bodegas of Jerez.

Olorosos, as the name implies, are sweet-scented full-bodied wines with a strong bouquet, a walnutty flavour and a dark gold or amber colour. Wine destined for oloroso is identified at an early stage and matured without the fino's flor. Pure olorosos are dry on the palate. Domecq's Rio Viejo is one of these rarer olorosos, being pure and dry like those prized in Spain.

Medium, Sweet, Cream and Brown are olorosos with increasing amounts of sweet Pedro Ximenez wine and colouring wine (fermented caramelised must) added to produce smooth, rich, dark sherries. Domecq's Celebration Cream is a full-bodied sweet oloroso, so called because it was created in 1935 to commemorate the Silver Jubilee of King George V of England. Venerable is a very sweet dessert wine of pure Pedro Ximenez, on average forty years old. It is often poured over vanilla and raisin ice cream or cake to make a delicious dessert.

A Palo Cortado is a rare and delicious style of sherry, sharing the characteristics of an oloroso and an amontillado. Domecq's Sibarita is a perfect example of this special wine: as the product of a solera that dates back to the historic year of 1792, it resembles an amontillado in aroma and an oloroso in body and smoothness.

Such a sybaritic, three-thousand-year-old pleasure as the unique fine wine of Jerez must have earned the few moments it takes to prepare its 'lid'. Whether this is a quickly set-out saucer of plump stuffed olives and a sliver of cheese, or a plate of slow-cooked herb-scented stew to enjoy at leisure, I hope the recipes in this book will encourage you to get the tapa habit. Then we may raise our glasses together in the traditional Spanish toast: 'Here's to health, love and wealth!' – 'Salud, amor y pesetas!'

Basics

Although tapas only officially appeared during the last century – they were first recorded in Seville – the tradition is part of a far older one: that of hospitality and the desire to honour a guest.

Algo para picar – something to nibble – always accompanies the offer of a glass of sherry in a Spanish household or bar. It is a matter of pride. Tapas are essentially small bits and pieces – quantity defines them, with quality dependent on the most freely-available local raw materials.

If there are snails at the bottom of your garden, snails is the tapa you will offer your guests. If the fishermen have returned with more sardines than they can sell, the local bar will serve grilled (broiled) sardines as the tapa. If the housewife made a good chick-pea stew yesterday, an honoured guest will be served a little saucer of that.

As well as these small opportunist snacks, there is a repertoire of everyday tapas, usually based on larder stores, which can range from a handful of salty biscuits to a dish of home-cured olives, from a plate of salt-cured ham cut from the family's Christmas treat, to a bit of good fresh country bread with savoury dripping.

Pickled olives
Aceitunas aliñadas

Spain exports large quantities of table olives, specialising in machine-pitted green olives stuffed with strips of pimento, whole almonds, tiny onions, or anchovies. Home-cured olives, *aceitunas aliñadas*, are the ones most frequently encountered in the tapa bars of the south.

Olives are a seasonal crop, gathered in the autumn in Andalucía when they are sold fresh, varying in size from fruit as large as a quail's egg to fruit smaller than a hazelnut, and varying in colour from bright green to pale mauve, depending on the degree of ripeness. In Spain, olives for pickling are harvested before they have a chance to ripen to black – the stage at which they are pressed for oil. The fresh fruits are cracked and soaked in pure water, or, if they are to be left whole, in water with lye (a leached solution), until they lose their bitterness. Then they are put in an earthenware crock with a loose wooden lid, to pickle submerged in a strong aromatic brine. Flavourings include herbs, garlic and wine vinegar, with sometimes a chilli or two, and maybe chunks of lemon or bitter orange to add flavour and piquancy. As the year wears on, the olives become sweeter and more pickled – until eventually they ferment. By which time the next year's crop will be ready. Those who do not pickle their own can select from a dozen or so different sizes and marinades on display in big plastic buckets in the market place.

A passable imitation of home-cured olives can be made by marinating commercially-prepared olives for a week or two in a home-made brine. I used to pickle my own fresh olives in this aromatic brine every year when I lived in Andalucía. Use the recipe as a guideline to make up your own spicing.

Makes 10 tapa portions

500 g (1 lb) can or jar of whole unpitted green olives	1 tablespoon coriander seeds
4 whole garlic cloves	1 dried fennel stick, broken into short lengths
1 lemon or bitter orange	1 small glass of sherry or wine vinegar
1–2 sprigs of thyme	

Drain the olives and bash them lightly with a rolling pin. Carefully burn the garlic in a naked flame until the papery cover blackens and drops off each one. Bash each clove once. Cut a slice from the middle of the lemon or orange and roughly chunk the rest.

Pack the olives, garlic and lemon or orange chunks (reserve the slice) in a screw-top jar, with the aromatics, vinegar and enough water to cover. Top with the lemon or orange slice to keep the olives submerged. You should not need extra salt – the conserved olives are usually salty enough.

Lid tightly and keep in the fridge for at least a week. Bring them up to room temperature to serve them.

Salted almonds
Almendras con sal

The Moors planted Spain's almond groves with stock from the Jordan valley – they found the fertile plain of Granada ideal for the cultivation of their favourite nut tree. Almonds are used extensively in Spanish cooking, both whole and ground, in sweetmeats and to thicken sauces. Every *feria* has its almond-salesman, every spice-merchant his store of almonds. There is nothing like the scent of freshly roasted almonds – for that alone, it's well worth preparing them yourself. They make a lovely squeak as you bite into them. Liberally dusted with salt, they give a fine thirst for the accompanying drink.

Makes 4 tapa portions

250g (8 oz) (1⅓ cups) almonds (in their skins or blanched) a little oil (optional)	1 teaspoon raw egg white, beaten lightly 1 tablespoon salt

Preheat the oven to Gas Mark 2/150°C/300°F. Roast the almonds, lightly slicked with oil, in the oven for 50–60 minutes until deliciously golden brown.

Alternatively, dry-fry the almonds gently in a heavy pan (skillet) until they take a fine roasted colour.

When they are done and piping hot, turn them in the beaten egg white – they will turn glossy. Then turn them in the salt. The salt will stick to the almonds, giving them a salty jacket which dries in their heat.

Serve them fresh and warm.

Spiced peanuts
Cacahuetes con sal picante

Salted nuts are a popular luxury on the tapa table. These days, almonds are often replaced by the cheaper, imported peanut.

Makes 4 tapa portions

250 g (8 oz) (1⅓ cups) peanuts (unskinned)
1 tablespoon oil
1 teaspoon paprika
¼ teaspoon cayenne pepper
½ teaspoon ground cumin
½ teaspoon ground coriander
1 teaspoon salt

Preheat the oven to Gas Mark 2/150°C/300°F.

Roast the peanuts for 60–75 minutes in the oven. They take longer to roast than most nuts – they should be pale gold.

Mix the peanuts with the oil and seasonings and return them to the oven for another 10 minutes, so the nuts absorb the oil and the heat develops the spices.

Serve them warm.

Toasted hazelnuts
Nueces tostadas

Hazelnuts are a wild crop in northern Spain. They are sometimes crushed and used in Catalan cooking to thicken sauces – instead of, or included with, ground almonds. They are served as tapas either plain roasted or roasted and salted. I like the simple rich flavour of the unsalted ones.

Makes 4 tapa portions

250 g (8 oz) (1⅓ cups) whole hazelnuts (skinned or unskinned)

Preheat the oven to Gas Mark 2/150°C/300°F.

Toast the hazelnuts in the oven for 50–60 minutes.

Serve the nuts warm. A dish of olives (page 14) and a plate of salty crisps (page 26) will complete a simple arrangement of tapas.

The La Ina solera system

A Spanish tapa feast

Cheese
Queso

Spain boasts a large range of cheeses, from the simplest of fresh curds to sophisticated matured blue-veined cheeses which can give Stilton and Roquefort a run for their money. Although there are many excellent local cheeses, only six have currently been granted Spain's official 'Denomination of Origin' which guarantees their quality. Any of these, served with bread and olives, make a delicious tapa. Manchego is the most widely available outside Spain.

Manchego, Spain's best-known cheese, is a mature hard ewe's milk cheese made on the high plateau of La Mancha in central Spain. It undergoes at least sixty days maturing, and the more expensive 'old' cheeses are left for considerably longer. The cylindrical cheeses weigh between four and eight kilos; they have a pale yellow rind flowered with a greenish-black mould when mature, and a characteristic plaited pattern round the sides. A whole cheese can be submerged in olive oil for further maturing – there is a tapa bar in Seville which specialises in this delicious strong-flavoured cheese. Buy the best and oldest Manchego you can afford to serve as a tapa. Cut it in thin slices just before you serve it.

Mahon, a cow's milk cheese from Minorca, can be eaten fresh or matured. It is drained in a linen cloth which gives it its characteristic fold-mark on the upper surface, and its square form with rounded edges. A whole cheese weighs between one and four kilos. Mahon cheese is served, in its home territory, cut in thin slices, dressed with olive oil and sprinkled with tarragon and pepper.

Idiazábal is, as its name suggests, a speciality of the Basque country. Made exclusively from ewe's milk, it is a whole cheese, cylindrical in shape with a golden rind and a compact pale ivory curd; it weighs between half and three-and-a-half kilos. It is sometimes smoked over beech and hawthorn wood, which gives the rind a dark brown colour and the cheese itself a deliciously smoky pungent flavour. Serve it cut into thin slivers, with bread.

Roncal is a pungent ewe's milk cheese made in the Roncal valley of Navarra – a high mountainous region whose sturdy independent inhabitants played a major part in Aragon's resistance to the Moors. A cylindrical cheese with a hard, straw-coloured rind and firm, slightly aerated texture, it is matured for at least four months. Roncal is only manufactured between December and July. Serve it cut into thin slivers, with bread and perhaps a finely-sliced raw sweet onion.

Cantabria is made exclusively with milk from Friesan cows in the Autonomous Community of Cantabria, where the climate is damp and the meadows are fertile enough to support the herds. The cheese is disc-shaped, with a soft bone-coloured rind and solid creamy texture. It is only lightly matured – for a minimum of seven days. Serve it cut into thin slices, with a few pickled gherkins as the accompaniment.

Cabrales comes from the isolated mountain valleys on the Asturian side of the Picos de Europa. Like its close cousin Picon, from the other side of the Picos, this is a fine piquant blue cheese made with a mixture of whole cow's milk and small proportions of goat's and/or ewe's milk. The cheese is ripened in traditional curing caves carved out of the mountainside, like those of Roquefort, for at least two months. It is marketed wrapped in the dried leaves of maple or plane trees. Locals sometimes mix the cheese with cider to make a powerful potted-cheese spread. To serve it as it is, cut it into small cubes.

Salt-cured ham
Jamón serrano

Jamón serrano, 'mountain ham', is the most valued of flavouring ingredients in Spanish cookery. In many kitchens, a whole haunch complete with trotter is often to be seen hanging alongside the obligatory string of dried red sweet peppers and the plait of garlic – although in poorer households this might only be at Christmas. There is always a stall in the market which deals in salted pig products, with a use for every little bit of the precious beast. The best cuts of ham are sliced off very finely to be served just as they are. The well-flavoured chewy little bits from near the bone are used to flavour soups, sauces and croquettes, or they might be fried with eggs, or go to flavour a tortilla; while the bones are sawn up to add richness, along with a piece of creamy yellow ham fat, to a bean stew.

Many rural households still keep a pig or two every year, to eat up the scraps and forage for acorns, roots and berries on the surrounding mountain slopes. I used to keep one for my own family when we lived in Andalucía. Slaughter is usually in the autumn, and if the pig-owner lives in a damp area by the sea, the hams will be sent up to a cousin or friend who lives in the mountains, to be cured in the cold dry air. From this custom has developed a commercial ham-curing industry, with certain mountain villages achieving particular fame for their product.

Jabugo in Huelva, Trevelez in Granada, Montanchez in Caceres, Sotoserrano and Candelario in the province of Salamanca are all well-known for their fine hams. Spain's Ministry of Agriculture has currently granted 'Denomination of Origin' status to the hams of the province of Teruel, and to those of Guijuelo, south east of Salamanca.

The ancient Iberian breed of near-wild pig makes the best serrano ham, in which flavour and body is more important than tenderness. Ham from the lean, rangy black or red Iberian pig which has been allowed to fatten on acorns and chestnuts in the wild, goes to make the prized *pata negra*. The cheaper hams are made with corralled beasts – either Landrace, Duroc or Large White – some of which have recently been successfully cross-bred with the native pigs.

Spanish 'mountain ham' is salt-cured and wind-dried without the application of heat or smoke. Its closest equivalent is Italian prosciutto. The initial dry-curing of the hams in salt lasts about ten days. After that they are hung up for the winter months in the rafters of an airy attic to cure in the cold dry winds of the *sierras*. When the weather turns warmer, the hams start to bead or sweat, and they are moved to a cool cellar to finish developing their characteristic flavour and texture. Free-range Iberian hams take longer to cure than those from corralled pigs, and are consequently much more expensive. They have very little exterior fat, a beautiful rich marbling of creamy fat throughout the meat, a wonderful deep red-wine colour and an incomparable wild-game flavour.

Makes 16 tapa mouthfuls   Allow 50–75 g (2–3 oz) per person as a starter

250 g (8 oz) jamón serrano   8 slices of country bread
or Parma ham

Wind-cured ham should be very finely sliced – almost transparent. Use a razor-sharp, long, slender, flexible blade such as those used for smoked salmon. The more freshly-sliced, the better it will be. Protect the cut surface of a ham, once started, with strips of its own fat (or greased tinfoil) so that it does not dry out. Serve with bite-sized pieces of bread – either separate or with the ham laid on as a topping.

Paprika sausage
Chorizo

At a rural pig-killing those meaty bits of the household pig which do not go for ham or bacon (*tocino*) are minced (ground) to make this garlic and paprika-spiced, all-meat sausage. Wind-dried and (sometimes, but not always) lightly smoked, chorizo is often prepared commercially in tandem with jamón serrano. These sausages are still made, along with black puddings, by rural housewives as part of their provision for winter. The rinsing and scrubbing of intestines for stuffing is one of the more leisurely activities of a country *matanza* (pig-killing) – ingenious modern cooks now use a hose-pipe instead of relying on the current of the stream to rinse out the insides of the long tubes.

The housewife makes her chorizo with roughly-chopped lean and fat pork. The meat is seasoned with salt, pepper, paprika, cumin, dried coriander, garlic and red wine, with maybe a bit of chilli or oregano. The mixture is stuffed into sausage casings, and then hung up to dry and cure. When making a Spanish stew, these seasonings, plus an all-pork sausage, will help to reproduce the flavour of Spanish chorizo.

Chorizo can be finished as single lengths, long loops, or knotted into short links of about 25–50 g (1–2 oz) a piece. When the chorizo is well-cured (firm and dark) it is often sliced and eaten raw, like Italian salami. The softer, less-cured sausages can be grilled (broiled) whole or sliced and fried as a deliciously piquant tapa. Well-cured tiny ones are delicious flamed in a little warmed brandy, which just singes the skin.

Other such speciality sausages include regional delicacies such as the rosemary-flavoured longaniza, and the Catalan butifarra and Valencian blanquets which replace the chorizo's paprika with cinnamon and nutmeg.

Makes 10–12 tapa mouthfuls   Serves 2–4 as a starter

250 g (8 oz) finely sliced mature chorizo sausage, or 375 g (12 oz) fresh chorizo, sliced thickly or twisted into single-mouthful lengths

10–12 small rounds of bread
oil or lard (shortening) for frying (optional)

If using the mature chorizo, cut the bread slices into quarters. Serve with the sliced raw chorizo.

If the chorizo is fresh, fry it in a drop of olive oil or lard (shortening) – it will soon yield its own fat – until brown and crisp outside but still juicy within. Serve either speared on to bread with cocktail sticks, or with bread fast-fried (but not saturated) in the fat which runs from the chorizo.

Black pudding
Morcilla

Rural Spanish housewives who still keep their own pigs, make their own black puddings with fresh pig's blood at the annual *matanza*. There was a time when all Europe's countrywomen made their own blood-sausages – each to her own regional recipe, including various seasonings, and sometimes barley or oats, rice or breadcrumbs, or whatever suited the climate and local habit.

Spain likes its blood-puddings flavoured with paprika, onions, garlic, cloves, pepper, marjoram, coriander and cumin. My neighbours in Andalucía included small cubes of lean pork and back-fat in their favourite mix – and in some districts rice is added as well. Simmering the loops of black-pudding in a cauldron over a wood-fire on the yard was the last chore of the *matanza*: when I asked my local mentor María how to tell when they were done, she told me they would sing when they were ready. Indeed they did, whistling air through the expanded tiny holes in the casing of intestine.

Makes 12–15 tapa mouthfuls   Serves 4 as a light meal (with eggs fried in the morcilla fat)

250 g (8 oz) Spanish
  morcilla, sliced thickly
OR
250 g (8 oz) black pudding
1–2 tablespoons olive oil or
  lard (shortening)
1 onion slice, chopped
  finely
1 garlic clove, crushed
1 teaspoon marjoram

1 teaspoon paprika
½ teaspoon ground cumin
¼ teaspoon ground cloves
½ teaspoon ground
  coriander
¼ teaspoon pepper

TO SERVE
12–15 bite-sized rounds of
  bread

If using the morcilla, fry or grill (broil) it in its own rich aromatic fat.

If using the black pudding, cut it into bite-sized pieces. Heat the oil or lard (shortening) in a frying pan (skillet). Fry the onion and garlic gently until soft and pale gold. Add the herbs and spices and the black pudding pieces. Fry the pieces until they are lightly crisp.

Serve hot, speared on to chunks of bread.

> *To experience the delicacy of fino wines at their best, they should be drunk chilled and from a freshly opened bottle.*

Pork drippings
Manteca de cerdo

There are three different flavours of pork dripping: white (sometimes perfumed with garlic and herbs); red (*colorada*) which is flavoured and coloured with paprika, and a paprika-coloured dripping in which small pieces of meat are preserved (a preparation rather like the French *rilletes*). These flavoured drippings can be bought at the pork-products stall in the market. They are popular as a labourer's breakfast, and any of the three drippings make good simple tapas, spread on bread, fresh or grilled (broiled). Here is an all-purpose paprika dripping with a little meat to give it interest. Use the skin from the meat to make scratchings (opposite).

Makes 8–10 tapa portions

250 g (8 oz) unsalted pork back-fat, cubed small
250 g (8 oz) belly pork, cubed small
2 tablespoons paprika
1 teaspoon dried thyme
1 teaspoon dried oregano
2–3 garlic cloves, singed and peeled
1 teaspoon salt

Preheat the oven to Gas Mark 1/140°C/275°F.

Put all the pork fat and belly in a large roasting tin and leave them in the oven for 5–6 hours, until the fat is all rendered. Stir in the spices, herbs and garlic and put it back in the oven to infuse for another hour.

Cool and store. Use as a spread on fresh or toasted bread.

Pork scratchings
Chicharros

These delicious little crisp-fried cracklings are strained out after the pork fat is rendered to make *manteca*. They are the traditional children's treat at the annual pig-killing – the *matanza* – which remains an important ritual in rural Spanish life.

Makes 6 tapa portions

125 g (4 oz) (½ cup) pure pork lard (shortening)
250 g (8 oz) pork skin, sliced into matchsticks

salt

Melt the lard (shortening) in a wide frying pan (skillet). When it is lightly hazed with blue, drop in the matchsticks of pork skin. They will puff up and brown crisp. Drain and sprinkle with salt. They keep well in an airtight tin.

Fresh sausages
Salchichas frescas

Spanish fresh sausages are spicy and made of pure pork. They can be a little fatty, so I prefer them fried or grilled (broiled) really crisp. Buy Toulouse sausages, or any all-meat sausage which has no rusk or breadcrumbs to bulk it out. Nutmeg is a popular sausage spicing in Spain, and all recipes include plenty of pepper and usually a little saltpetre to turn them bacon-pink.

Makes 20–25 tapa mouthfuls   Serves 4 as a starter   (Pictured on page 143)

500 g (1 lb) all-meat pork sausages (Toulouse are fine)
1 tablespoon olive oil or lard (shortening)
1 garlic clove, crushed (optional)

½ teaspoon grated nutmeg
salt and pepper
fresh tomato sauce (page 101), to serve

Twist the sausages into bite-sized lengths – as long as a joint of your thumb. Fry them in the oil or lard (shortening) until crisp and well-browned, with the garlic, if they were not garlicked already. Sprinkle with the nutmeg, and salt and pepper.
Serve piping hot, with fresh tomato sauce.

Hot bread with olive oil and garlic
Pan con aceite y ajo

Spanish country bread is excellent, and many Andalucían villages still boast a village baker to supply the most important staple of the rural diet. Close textured and always creamy-white, with a crisp golden-brown crust, country bread is usually sour-dough, with each batch raised with a starter from the day before. This, plus the precise mix and grind of the flour used, and still in some cases the wood used to heat the oven, gives an individual flavour to the product of different bakers. Such bread is sold by weight – value for money is of the essence. The comparative merits of, say, the bread of Facinas and the bread of Pelayo, were a keen subject for discussion in my local bar.

Bread with garlic and oil is a favourite Andaluz breakfast, and provides the simplest of tapas – perfect basic materials are all that is required.

Makes about 8–10 slices

500 g (1 lb) close-textured country bread (home-made is best)
1 garlic clove, cut in half

4–5 tablespoons extra virgin olive oil
salt

Warm the bread through in the oven. Cut it in thick slices and rub each slice with the cut garlic glove. Trickle warm olive oil on to each slice and sprinkle with salt. That's it!

Potato crisps
Patatas fritas

These can be bought hot from the fryer on many a street corner, being a spin-off from Spain's favourite breakfast, *churros* (doughnut-like fritters). All morning long the frying-kiosks are kept busy supplying everyone – from grannies to schoolchildren to business-men – with their morning ration of *churros*, to be enjoyed in a nearby café with hot milky coffee or chocolate. In the evening the kiosk-cooks use the same equipment to fry crisps, which are also taken to the local café, this time to be enjoyed with a glass of wine.

Makes 6 tapa portions

1 kg (2 lb) old potatoes
oil for deep-frying (olive with sunflower is perfect)
salt

Wash the potatoes well, dry them thoroughly, and cut them into near-transparent slices (you can peel them if you wish).

Heat the oil until it is hazed with blue. Deep-fry the slices, a handful at a time so that the oil temperature does not drop. Drain on kitchen paper and sprinkle with salt.

You won't regret the effort of making your own.

Canapés of conserved tuna

Canapes de atún en conserva

Conserved tuna fish is a traditional larder-store all round the Mediterranean. The inshore fleet of Algeciras, for many years my local market-port, supplied a vigorous local tuna-canning industry until the recent depletion of stocks made the activity uneconomic.

Tuna is also salt-dried very much like cod, particularly round Valencia. The method yields *mojama* (middle-cut of tuna, salted and dried) and *huevas* (salted, dried roe). Both are expensive luxury tapas, served very thinly sliced and dressed with a trickle of olive oil.

Canned tuna is a more everyday pleasure. Serve the flaked, drained fish any way you please. Try it plain with bread and a small dish of olives (page 14), or dressed with a spoonful of mayonnaise (page 31) and a strip of red pepper. Or, as here, on lettuce leaves.

Makes 8–10 tapa mouthfuls   Serves 2 as a starter   (Pictured on page 108)

198 g (7 oz) can of tuna fish in brine or oil
1 tablespoon finely chopped mild onion
1 tablespoon chopped parsley
8–10 bite-sized pieces of cos lettuce leaves
2–3 tablespoons olive oil
salt and pepper

Drain the tuna fish and flake it lightly with the onion and parsley. Arrange the lettuce leaves on a plate.

Divide the tuna between the lettuce leaves. Dress with a trickle of oil and a sprinkle of salt and pepper.

Salt cod with chilli
Pericana

Bacalao (salt cod) was an essential storecupboard item throughout the Mediterranean during the Middle Ages, when Roman Catholics observed more than half the year as fasting. It remains popular even when fresh fish is on offer. This is a dish from the shepherding villages in the mountains behind Valencia, where *bacalao* is called 'mountain fish'. Choose firm white salt cod without any yellow tinge – the middle cut is the best. *Pericana* should be served with a *coca*, a Valencian unleavened bread much like pitta.

Makes 15–20 tapa mouthfuls   Serves 4 as a starter

250 g (8 oz) salt cod, soaked in fresh water for 48 hours to de-salt
½ head of garlic
2 red sweet peppers (or dried red sweet peppers, deep-fried)
2 tablespoons olive oil
¼ teaspoon cayenne pepper
2–3 unleavened breads (pitta or nan, to replace coca), to serve

Dry the salt cod well, remove any bones, and trim it into manageable pieces for grilling (broiling).

Carefully hold the head of garlic in a direct flame and burn off the papery outside. Peel the cloves. Turn the peppers in the flame until the skin blisters black. Skin, hull and de-seed the peppers.

Heat a heavy iron pan (skillet) or griddle until it is smoking hot. Put on the garlic cloves. Blister the salt cod on a high heat, turning once, until its edges blacken.

Skin the cod and tear it into small flakes with the fingers – no nonsense with knives. Tear the peppers into strips. Chop the garlic. Toss all the ingredients together. Sprinkle with the olive oil and a little cayenne pepper to add extra bite. Leave to infuse for half an hour or so.

Accompany with hot pitta or any unleavened bread.

Canned sardines with onion
Sardinas en conserva con cebolla

Sardines are an excellent instant tapa, served plain or mashed with a little mayonnaise (page 31), spread on toast and topped with a strip of pimento. I like them on grilled bread with a little onion to cut the oiliness of the fish. A standard small can of sardines contains three to five fish.

Makes 6–10 tapa mouthfuls   Serves 2 as a starter   (Pictured on page 108)

120 g (4 oz) can of sardines (in oil or tomato sauce)
½ sweet onion, sliced finely

6–8 small pieces of grilled (broiled) bread
a little olive oil (optional)
salt and pepper

Fillet the sardines horizontally. Remove the backbone if you prefer (I like its crunchiness).

Lay a few rings of onion on each piece of grilled (broiled) bread. Rural Spanish housewives toast bread on a metal plate topped with a hinged grill, which goes over a direct flame. It gives deliciously charred soft toast, rather than the smooth all-over tan of a toaster.

Top the onion with half a sardine, skin-side up. Sprinkle with salt and pepper, the oil or tomato sauce from the can and a trickle of extra oil, if wished.

> *A tapa portion generally consists of two mouthfuls, and it is served on a small oval plate or saucer. More expensive dishes, or larger servings, are served as a whole 'ration'. This makes up a plateful, which is a small dinner plate crammed to capacity. Half-a-ration is a side plate full. Quantity is dictated by plate-size – a small amount of food is never served in the middle of a large plate, as the aim is to appear generous and hospitable.*

3

Salads and cold dishes

A wide variety of cold dishes and substantial salads are the mainstay of the tapa table all over Spain. Less varied than the hot dishes, they back up the specialities of the house. They serve a double function: ready-prepared, they can be served immediately; in addition they offer an economical vehicle for the surplus from the restaurant. At home, these little salads can be made with small quantities of leftovers, and the advance preparation they require makes them ideal cold starters to a meal.

In the tapa bar, there are a few old favourites without which no selection would be considered complete. These vary from region to region, but in the south they include a cold potato tortilla (page 66), fresh-pickled anchovies, dressed artichoke hearts, and egg mayonnaise.

Cold cooked vegetables are transformed as a mayonnaise-coated Russian salad (very popular as a free tapa) or in a potato salad. Most bars offer a mixed fish salad dressed with oil and vinegar – a dish which accommodates any ready-cooked shellfish and crustaceans which remain unsold at the end of the day, and whose flavour is enhanced by a night's marination.

Any of these dishes, alone or in combination, make excellent first courses. Two or three served together with a green salad make a light summer lunch.

Russian salad with mayonnaise
Ensalada rusa a la mahonesa

This is the standby of every tapa bar, and it's often dressed with home-made mayonnaise. The making of this famous sauce is a skill which comes easily to Spanish housewives, who maintain that it has its origins in Mahon, Menorca. It cannot be made in really small quantities – a one-egg-yolk sauce is the minimum. Store any extra in a screw-top jar in the fridge, and, once it has cooled, don't beat it again even if it looks like separating.

You can, of course, use ready-cooked vegetables in the dish, and vary the combinations. Once made, it keeps for at least two to three days in a covered container in the fridge.

Makes 15–20 tapa mouthfuls   Serves 2 as a starter   (Pictured on page 53)

THE VEGETABLES
1 large carrot, diced small
1 small turnip, diced small
1 large potato, diced small
2 tablespoons green beans,
    cut into short lengths
2 tablespoons shelled peas
1 tablespoon wine vinegar
1 tablespoon olive oil
salt

THE MAYONNAISE
1 egg yolk
150 ml (¼ pint) (⅔ cup)
    olive oil
1 tablespoon sherry or
    wine vinegar
salt

TO SERVE
lettuce leaves (optional)

Cook the vegetables in boiling salted water, adding them in the order in which they are listed. As soon as they are soft (8–10 minutes for the carrot and turnip which need longest), drain and splash them under cold water. Coat them with the vinegar and oil and a little salt.

Make the mayonnaise while the vegetables cool. Put the egg yolk in a deep plate and beat it with a fork. Very slowly trickle in the oil, drop by drop at first, beating steadily with the fork. As the sauce thickens, so you can increase the trickle – if the egg yolk is small, it will not accept all the oil. If it looks like splitting, fork furiously at one little corner until you get the sauce smooth and thick again, and then work in the rest. Finish with the vinegar and a little salt.

Alternatively, make the mayonnaise in a food processor, using the egg white as well as the egg yolk.

Turn the cooled vegetables in enough mayonnaise to coat them. Serve a teaspoonful in individual saucers with forks, or in small lettuce leaves.

Potato mayonnaise with red sweet peppers
Patatas a la mahonesa

This simple salad is delicious made with leftover baked potatoes. A few chopped gherkins make a good addition, and the red sweet pepper can be replaced with a sprinkle of paprika (the same vegetable dried and ground to a powder). This dish can be prepared two or three days in advance and kept in a covered container in the fridge.

Makes 12–15 tapa mouthfuls   Serves 2 as a starter   (Pictured on page 71)

2 large cooked potatoes, skinned and diced
2 tablespoons olive oil
1 teaspoon sherry or wine vinegar
3–4 tablespoons mayonnaise (page 31)

2–3 strips of red sweet pepper
salt and pepper
small lettuce leaves, to serve (optional)

Toss the diced potatoes with the oil, vinegar, and salt and pepper – best done while the potatoes are still hot.

When the potatoes are quite cool, coat them with the mayonnaise and decorate with the strips of red sweet pepper.

Serve the potato mayonnaise either in individual saucers with forks, or spooned into small lettuce leaves – these make neat edible containers for sloppy tapas.

Prawns with mayonnaise
Cóctel de gambas

The ubiquitous prawn cocktail turns up regularly on the Spanish menu. Since it combines Spain's two great culinary strengths – excellent fresh shellfish and home-made mayonnaise – it can be very good. This version comes from the Campo de Gibraltar, where Worcestershire sauce has long been a favourite in the local bars. Make it up as you need it – this is not a dish which keeps well.

Makes 8–10 tapa mouthfuls   Serves 2 as a starter

125 g (4 oz) cooked peeled
  prawns
3 tablespoons mayonnaise
  (page 31)
½ teaspoon paprika
1 teaspoon Worcestershire
  sauce

1 teaspoon tomato purée
1 teaspoon gin
salt and pepper
lettuce leaves or cherry
  tomatoes, to serve

Pick over the prawns and drain them thoroughly if they
were frozen. Combine the mayonnaise with the paprika,
Worcestershire sauce, tomato purée and gin. Taste and
adjust the seasoning if necessary. Dress the prawns with this
sauce.

Serve spooned into small lettuce leaves or tiny hollowed-
out tomatoes, each speared with a cocktail stick.

Eggs with mayonnaise
Huevos con mahonesa

This is a favourite of tapa bars. The quality is dependent upon the
raw materials – if the mayonnaise is home-made, and the eggs just
gathered from underneath a barnyard hen, there is no finer dish.

Makes 16 tapa mouthfuls   Serves 4 as a starter   (Pictured on page 126)

4 small eggs (size 4)
4 tablespoons mayonnaise
  (page 31)

1–2 strips of cooked red
  sweet pepper or ½
  teaspoon paprika

Start the eggs in cold water and bring them gently to the
boil. Take the pan off the heat, lid it and leave them in the
water for 6–8 minutes to set the yolks. Plunge the eggs into
cold water to loosen the shell. Peel them, halve them and
arrange them on a plate.

Dress each egg-half with ½ teaspoon of the mayonnaise
and a scrap of the red sweet pepper or a pinch of paprika.
(This is the moment when the icing nozzle usually comes
into play in the grander tapa bars.)

If serving as a first course, the eggs can be presented on a
large dish. For a tapa, serve each egg-half cut in half again
and speared with a cocktail stick.

Note: the yolks can be taken out and mashed up with a little
oil, a pinch of ground cumin and an anchovy or two if you
are not perfectly confident that your eggs are of the best.

Cherry tomatoes mimosa
Tomatitos a la mimosa

This is a quickly prepared tapa which takes advantage of those tiny cherry tomatoes which might have been specially grown for the purpose. It's just as good, although not as pretty, made with the larger ones. This can be assembled a few hours ahead.

Makes 8–10 tapa mouthfuls   Serves 2 as a starter   (Pictured on page 143)

8–10 cherry tomatoes
1 hard-boiled egg
2–3 anchovy fillets

8 green olive slices
1–2 tablespoons olive oil

Cut the top off each little tomato and scoop out the middle, discarding the flesh. Chop the egg finely. Chop the anchovies with the tomato tops.

Stuff the tomato shells with the anchovy mixture and then the olive slices, and then top with the chopped hard-boiled egg. Finish with a trickle of the olive oil and spear each tomato with a cocktail stick before serving.

Cod's roe salad
Ensalada de huevas de merluza

This is one of my favourite tapa salads. Hake roe is often used for the dish in Spain. The dressing is also good on leftover cooked mussels and shellfish. It keeps for four to five days in the fridge.

Makes 12–15 tapa mouthfuls   Serves 2 as a starter   (Pictured on page 125)

1 wing of cooked cod's roe
1 tablespoon chopped
  spring onion
1 tablespoon chopped red
  sweet pepper
1 garlic clove, chopped

1 teaspoon chopped
  parsley
3–4 tablespoons olive oil
1 tablespoon sherry or
  wine vinegar
salt and pepper

Skin and dice the cod's roe into 1 cm (½-inch) cubes. Mix the rest of the ingredients together and pour them over the roe. Turn the pieces gently in the marinade, taking care not to break them up. Leave in a cool place or the fridge to marinate for a few hours or overnight.

Serve one piece of roe per tapa portion, with a little of the marinade poured over and plenty of bread to mop up the juices.

*The Andalucían market place: the fruit stall; the snail stall;
the delicatessen; the vegetable stall*

Unloading the catch in Sanlúcar de Barrameda
and selling it in and around the markets of Jerez

Fresh pickled anchovies
Boquerones en vinagre

The fresh anchovy looks like a small slender sardine – both fish are a plentiful catch on the southern coasts of Spain. This preparation, in pre-refrigeration days, provided a simple method of adding a little shelf-life to small fish which could not be eaten fresh. It's so good it has remained on the tapa menu ever since. Start forty-eight hours ahead – maybe when you have a handful of fish left over from frying (page 83). The preparation keeps for four to five days in the fridge.

Makes 10–12 tapa mouthfuls   Serves 2 as a starter

250 g (8 oz) fresh anchovies or sprats	2 tablespoons water
1–2 garlic cloves, sliced	1 tablespoon olive oil
150 ml (¼ pint) (⅔ cup) sherry or wine vinegar	1 teaspoon chopped parsley
	salt and pepper

Rinse the anchovies – they have no scales to worry about; sprats will have to be checked for scales. Gut the little fish with your finger through the soft belly. Pull the head of each fish firmly down through the belly towards the tail. This will bring the spine with it and leave the fish split in a butterfly, all in one movement. Otherwise, cut them in half with a sharp knife and remove the backbone.

Lay the opened fish flesh upwards in a single layer in a shallow dish. Sprinkle with the garlic, and salt and pepper. Mix the vinegar with the water (sherry vinegar is powerful stuff) and pour it over.

Cover with foil and leave in the fridge to marinate for 48 hours. Finish with a slick of the olive oil and a sprinkle of the parsley.

Serve one fish per tapa, with a chunk of bread and cocktail sticks.

Sherry vinegar is a fine, oak-flavoured strong vinegar which adds richness and distinction to a dish. It must be used sparingly and diluted with water if the dish calls for a large volume of liquid. Balsamic vinegar is the Italian equivalent. Substitute wine vinegar – white or red – if you cannot get either.

Asparagus with two sauces
Espárragos con dos salsas

Mayonnaise and fresh-flavoured chopped-vegetable sauce often turn up as an accompaniment to grilled fish steaks. The vegetable sauce was a particular favourite in my local bar in Tarifa, where it seemed to appear with everything, including a bit of bread for dunking; in the winter it sauced a baked potato.

Makes 8 tapa mouthfuls   Serves 1 as a starter

8 cooked asparagus spears, well-drained and cooled
2–3 tablespoons mayonnaise (page 31)

CHOPPED VEGETABLE SAUCE
1 small tomato, chopped finely
½ green pepper, chopped finely
2–3 cocktail gherkins, chopped finely

½ onion, chopped finely
1 tablespoon chopped parsley
4 tablespoons olive oil
2 tablespoons sherry or wine vinegar
1 garlic clove, chopped finely (optional)
salt and pepper

Trim off the woody ends of the asparagus.

Mix together all the ingredients for the chopped vegetable sauce.

Serve each asparagus spear flanked with a teaspoon of mayonnaise and a teaspoon of chopped vegetable sauce.

Red sweet peppers in oil
Pimientos en aceite

This preparation is worth making in larger quantities as it keeps for a couple of weeks in the fridge. It's my own favourite larder standby – not only is it delicious on its own, it is also very useful for decorating other tapas. Store it in a screw-top jar, topped up with olive oil so that the peppers are submerged. Any leftover oil is delicious trickled over a potato salad, or used in a seafood mayonnaise.

Makes 12–15 tapa mouthfuls   Serves 2 as a starter

| 2 large red sweet peppers | 1 garlic clove, sliced |
| 6 tablespoons olive oil | cubes of bread, to serve |

Hull and de-seed the peppers and cut them into strips.

Warm the oil in a small frying pan (skillet). Add the peppers and stew them gently until they are soft and the juices have evaporated so that the oil is once again clear. (As the oil heats up, the sugar in the peppers caramelises, which gives the finished dish a lovely roasted flavour.) Throw in the garlic at the last minute – it should soften but not brown. Take the peppers off the heat, and tip the contents of the pan into a small dish to cool.

Cut the pepper strips into bite-sized pieces. Serve them in their garlic-flavoured oil, speared on to cubes of bread with cocktail sticks. This is the most delectable of finger-food.

Artichokes in oil
Alcachofas en aceite

This is a very common tapa in the south of Spain, where artichokes are plentiful and cheap. It can be made with canned artichoke hearts.

Makes 4 tapa portions   Serves 2 as a starter   (Pictured on page 54)

4 small cooked artichokes	1 spring onion, chopped
or artichoke hearts	finely
6 tablespoons olive oil	salt and pepper
1 garlic clove, chopped	
finely	

Arrange the artichokes on a deep plate into which you have trickled a little of the oil. If the artichokes are whole, trim the leaves right down to the tender base without pulling them away, and carefully cut out the choke (the nest of hairy little leaves at the heart).

Mix the garlic and spring onion with the remaining oil, and salt and pepper. Pour this dressing into the artichoke hearts.

Note: finely chopped peppers, egg, tomato or cucumber can be mixed into the dressing if you have any left over from another tapa dish.

New potato salad
Ensalada de patatas frescas

This is my household's favourite summer lunch – a conveniently pre-cooked feast which sits in a large dish on the table all day for the sustenance of passing hungry teenagers. The leftovers make good little tapas in the evening.

Makes 20–24 tapa mouthfuls   Serves 2 as a main course (with croûtons and bacon)   (Pictured on page 54)

500 g (1 lb) new potatoes, cooked in their skins
4 tablespoons olive oil
1 tablespoon sherry or wine vinegar
1 tablespoon diced cucumber
1 tablespoon diced green pepper
1 tablespoon diced red sweet pepper
1 tablespoon chopped onion (spring onion is excellent)

1 hard-boiled egg, chopped roughly
3–4 anchovy fillets, chopped
6–8 black olives
salt and pepper
hot croûtons (fried in olive oil and garlic) and crisp fried bacon, to serve (optional)

Toss the potatoes with the oil, vinegar, and salt and pepper while they're still hot. When the potatoes have cooled a little, mix in the rest of the ingredients.

For a more substantial dish, top just before serving with hot fried croûtons and crisp fried bacon.

Serve with forks in individual dishes or on one large serving plate.

Rice salad with pine kernels
Ensalada de arroz con pinoñes

Prepared in larger quantities, this Valencian rice salad is excellent with cold chicken or ham. If serving it to accompany a meal, allow 75 g (3 oz) (½ cup) uncooked weight of rice per person (double these quantities for cooked rice).

Makes 15–20 tapa mouthfuls   Serves 3–4 as a starter or to accompany cold meat   (Pictured on page 107)

8 heaped tablespoons
  cooked rice
1 tablespoon toasted pine
  kernels or slivered
  almonds
1 tablespoon cooked peas
1 tablespoon chopped
  apple
1 tablespoon chopped
  green pepper

1 tablespoon chopped red
  sweet pepper
3 tablespoons olive oil
1 tablespoon lemon juice
salt
chicory leaves, to serve
  (optional)

Toss all the ingredients lightly together. Serve in individual
saucers with small forks. Alternatively, serve spooned into
chicory leaves (conveniently boat-shaped), with a cocktail
stick speared into each.

Rice salad with tuna fish

Ensalada de arroz con atún en conserva

Leftover rice is the basis for this salad. In Spain the usual rice is
round – similar to our pudding rice. Long-grain rice will do as well.
It's a good standby for a buffet – particularly to accompany cold
seafood such as prawns, lobster or salmon with mayonnaise. For a
full portion, allow about 75 g (3 oz) (½ cup) uncooked weight of rice
per person (double these quantities for cooked rice).

*Makes 15–20 tapa mouthfuls Serves 3–4 as a starter or to accompany
seafood*

8 heaped tablespoons
  cooked rice
1 tablespoon chopped
  green pepper
1 tablespoon chopped
  onion
1 tablespoon chopped
  cucumber
1 tablespoon chopped
  parsley

1 tablespoon flaked tuna
  fish
4 tablespoons olive oil
1 tablespoon lemon juice
salt and pepper
small lettuce leaves, to
  serve (optional)

Toss all the ingredients lightly together and serve in little
dishes with forks, or spooned into small lettuce leaves.

41

Beetroot salad
Ensalada de remolacha

Look for fresh-cooked beetroot which hasn't been sodden in vinegar for this fresh-flavoured salad. There is no salt or vinegar in the seasoning – the garlic gives it enough bite. It can be prepared a day or two ahead and left to marinate in the fridge.

Makes 12–15 tapa mouthfuls   Serves 2 as a starter   (Pictured on page 108)

250g (8oz) cooked beetroot, skinned and sliced
1 garlic clove, chopped
1 tablespoon chopped parsley
2 tablespoons olive oil
pepper

Lay the beetroot slices in a shallow dish. Sprinkle over the rest of the ingredients. Leave to marinate for an hour or two, or overnight.

Serve cut into bite-sized pieces, with cocktail sticks or forks for easy handling.

Salad kebabs
Pinchos de ensalada mixta

The Spanish mixed salad is as variable as the market garden can make it. Apart from artichoke hearts, it doesn't usually include cooked vegetables – they go into *ensalada rusa* (page 31). Otherwise, anything goes. It makes an excellent start to a summer meal – a kind of Spanish *salade niçoise*. When serving it as a tapa, spear the ingredients, kebab-style, on a cocktail stick to make a *pincho*.

Makes 16 tapa mouthfuls   Serves 2 as a starter   (Pictured on page 72)

2–3 cos lettuce leaves, sliced across the stalk
1 small tomato, cut into 8
8 small cubes of cucumber
8 anchovy-stuffed green olives
1 slice of mild onion or 1 spring onion, cut into pieces
1 cooked artichoke heart, cut into 8
1 small red sweet or green pepper, hulled, de-seeded and chopped into 8
½ hard-boiled egg, chopped finely
3 tablespoons olive oil
a squeeze of lemon juice
salt

Thread the lettuce, tomato, cucumber, olives, onion, artichoke and pepper on to 8 cocktail sticks, kebab-style. Sprinkle on the chopped hard-boiled egg, oil and lemon juice and a little salt.

Chicory and blue cheese
Chicoría con queso de cabrales

This is a very common tapa in the north of Spain, where the French influence is strong. The filling is often the blue-veined Cabrales, matured wrapped in chestnut leaves, which is made in Asturias. It has a chalky texture and flavour like Roquefort.

Makes 8 tapa mouthfuls   Serves 2 as a starter   (Pictured on page 126)

8 chicory leaves
125 g (4 oz) blue cheese
  (Cabrales, Roquefort,
  Danish Blue or Stilton)

2 tablespoons soured
  cream or thick yogurt
1 teaspoon paprika

Wipe the chicory leaves and arrange them on a plate. Mash the cheese with the cream or yogurt.
  Stuff the leaves with the cheese mixture. Finish with a sprinkle of the paprika and a cocktail stick for easy handling.

Tomatoes with anchovies
Tomates con anchoas

This is a classic combination in Spain. Anchovies are still sold straight from the barrel in rural general stores. If they are bought loose, the whiskery little fish have to be boned and soaked in milk before using – canned ones are much easier.

Makes 8–10 tapa mouthfuls   Serves 2 as a starter   (Pictured on page 108)

1 large ripe beef tomato
100 g (3½ oz) can of
  anchovies in oil

8–10 pimento-stuffed
  olives
pepper

Wipe and slice the tomato and arrange the slices on a plate in a single layer. Roll the anchovy fillets and place one on each tomato slice. Top with a stuffed olive and a trickle of oil from the can. Sprinkle with pepper.

Seafood salad
Ensalada de mariscos

The ingredients for this vary with the local catch. All shellfish and crustaceans (except crab, which is not firm enough) are welcome. Make up your own combinations. If these are lacking, increase the proportion of cucumber and green pepper and add a few cubes of cold potato. It makes a good first course, served on shredded lettuce.

Makes 20–24 tapa mouthfuls   Serves 4 as a starter   (Pictured on page 72)

2 tablespoons prawns, cooked and peeled (fresh or frozen)
2 tablespoons clams or cockles, cooked and shelled (fresh or canned)
2 tablespoons mussels, cooked and shelled (fresh or canned)
2 tablespoons stewed squid (page 94)
1 tablespoon chopped green pepper
1 tablespoon chopped cucumber
1 tablespoon chopped onion
1 tablespoon chopped parsley
5 tablespoons olive oil
2 tablespoons sherry or wine vinegar
½ teaspoon coriander seeds
salt and pepper
small lettuce leaves, to serve (optional)

Combine all the ingredients and leave them to marinate overnight.

Serve either in small individual dishes with forks, or on little lettuce leaves spiked with cocktail sticks.

Tomatoes with garlic and marjoram
Tomates con ajo y mejorana

Choose a ripe tomato and firm fresh garlic for this simple combination: its success depends on good raw materials freshly prepared. Onion and parsley can be substituted for the marjoram and garlic.

Makes 8–10 tapa mouthfuls   Serves 1–2 as a starter   (Pictured on page 72)

1 large ripe beef tomato	1–2 tablespoons olive oil
1 garlic clove	a pinch of granulated sugar
1 teaspoon marjoram leaves	pepper

Wipe and slice the tomato. Arrange the slices on a plate in a single layer. Slice the garlic very finely. Scatter the garlic and marjoram leaves over the tomatoes. Trickle on the olive oil and finish with pepper and a sprinkle of sugar.

Red sweet pepper and tuna fish casserole
Pote

I first tasted this delicious combination in Mora de Toledo in La Mancha – where they grow the finest and fattest of red sweet peppers. Mora is a little whitewashed town set in the red earth of the central plateau's olive groves. The harvest is late up on the high plain, production small but high quality – particularly the greeny-gold first-pressing virgin oils. This dish can be prepared a day or two ahead.

Makes 10–12 tapa mouthfuls   Serves 2 as a starter

2 large red sweet peppers	1 hard-boiled egg, sliced
6 tablespoons virgin olive oil	198 g (7 oz) can of tuna fish in oil, drained and flaked
1–2 garlic cloves, crushed	pepper
1 teaspoon dried thyme	

Preheat the oven to Gas Mark 8/230°C/450°F.

Using a long toasting fork carefully blister the peppers over a direct flame, or under the grill, until the skin blackens and peels off easily (I sometimes omit this step). Hull and de-seed the peppers, and slice them into strips.

Trickle a little of the oil into 2 small shallow earthenware casseroles or 1 larger baking dish, and lay in the strips of pepper. Trickle the rest of the oil over them.

Cook in the oven for 15–20 minutes until the peppers are sizzling. Sprinkle with the garlic and thyme and leave to cool.

When you are ready to serve, sprinkle over the slices of hard-boiled egg, the flakes of tuna and a little pepper.

Serve with chunks of bread and little forks for sharing from the cooking dish.

Vegetables

Spain has an excellent choice of good vegetables. Markets are particularly strong, of course, in Mediterranean varieties that need plenty of sunshine to ripen to perfection – peppers, aubergines (eggplants), artichokes and tomatoes among them.

All our own familiar northern vegetables grow very well in the fertile climate and make their appearance on the tapa table, including green beans and broad beans, potatoes and carrots, and leeks and onions. Less familiar vegetables include a variety of wild greens such as *tagarnina* – the leaf-rosette of a large thistle – and wild-gathered asparagus sprue; and in winter Swiss chard and cardoons (a winter-maturing member of the artichoke family). Unlike their neighbours the French, the Spanish are suspicious of their wild fungi. Three main varieties are picked: our own familiar field mushrooms, oyster mushrooms, and saffron milkcaps (bright orange fungi which bruise blue and are a favourite autumn tapa in the bars of Valencia).

Vegetables in Spain are often served separately at the beginning of the meal. Any of the following recipes make a delicious first course.

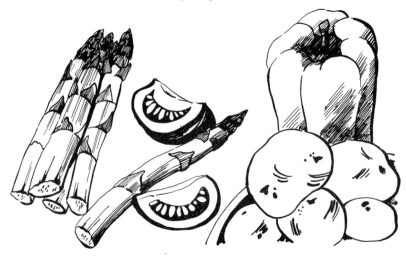

Grilled (broiled) mushrooms with garlic and rosemary
Champiñones a la parrilla

I have included rosemary in this recipe to give the flavour of the Andalucían *maquis* (scrub-covered hills), where mushrooms are a wild-gathered crop in autumn and spring. As well as the usual damp meadows, they seem to spring up in the charred wake of forest fires.

Makes 8 tapa mouthfuls   Serves 2 as a starter

250 g (8 oz) mushrooms (flat or well-grown buttons)
1–2 fat garlic cloves

1 teaspoon dried rosemary
2 tablespoons olive oil
salt and pepper
bread squares, to serve

Wipe the mushrooms and trim the stalks level with the caps. Discard the trimmings. Arrange the mushrooms stalk upwards on a grill (broiling) pan or griddle.

Chop the garlic finely. Sprinkle the mushroom caps with the chopped garlic, rosemary, olive oil and salt and pepper.

Grill (broil) the mushrooms fiercely until the juices run and the caps are spitting hot. Serve on squares of fresh bread, each speared with a cocktail stick.

Baked potatoes with oil and onion
Patatas con cebolla

A substantial tapa for a cold winter evening; this dish is from the mountains of Huesca.

Makes 4 large tapa portions   Serves 4 as a starter

4 medium-size potatoes
1 mild onion (Spanish), chopped finely

6 tablespoons olive oil
salt and pepper

Preheat the oven to Gas Mark 5/190°C/375°F.

Scrub the potatoes and bake them in the oven for an hour, until the flesh is soft and the skin crisp.

Mix the chopped onion with the olive oil and salt and pepper.

Open up the potatoes and spoon in the oil and onion mixture. Eat them hot, one each per tapa.

Baked mushrooms with parsley and garlic
Setas al horno

This simple way of preparing cultivated mushrooms is also delicious with other fungi – particularly oyster mushrooms and small cepes. In Valencia it is a favourite recipe for wild-gathered saffron milkcaps.

Makes 8–10 tapa mouthfuls   Serves 2 as a starter   (Pictured on page 54)

250 g (8 oz) mushrooms (small open ones are best for this)
4 tablespoons olive oil
1 garlic clove, chopped
1 heaped tablespoon chopped parsley
2 heaped tablespoons fresh breadcrumbs
salt and pepper

Preheat the oven to Gas Mark 6/200°C/400°F.

Wipe the mushrooms but do not peel or wash them. Trim off the stalks close to the caps. Arrange the caps in a shallow ovenproof dish which will just accommodate them, and tuck the stalks into the gaps. Trickle the oil over and around the mushrooms and sprinkle them with salt and pepper. Bake in the oven for 20–25 minutes.

Meanwhile fork the garlic, parsley and breadcrumbs lightly together. After the mushrooms have been cooking for 10 minutes, top them with the mixture. Baste the topping with the mushroom juices and return the dish to the oven for the remaining 10–15 minutes.

Serve the mushrooms sizzling hot, if possible in their cooking dish.

Aubergine (eggplant) purée
Pez de tierra

The Spanish name for this purée is 'earth fish'. I had it first in Peniscola, where the last of the Avignon Popes spent his final days. It's a fast-day dish – important in Catholic Spain where in medieval times more than half the year was a fast. The ingredients were considerably cheaper than *pez de monte* (mountain fish) – the nickname given to the alternative fasting-food, *bacalao* (salt cod).

Makes 10–12 tapa mouthfuls   Serves 2 as a starter   (Pictured on page 54)

1 large firm aubergine (eggplant)	6 tablespoons olive oil
3 garlic cloves	½ teaspoon ground cumin
	salt and pepper

Wipe, hull and cut the aubergine (eggplant) into chunks – don't bother with the salting and rinsing so often advocated. Chop the garlic roughly.

Heat the oil in a shallow pan (skillet). Add the garlic and cook it for a minute or two. Add the chunked aubergine (eggplant). Fry, turning as each side cooks, until the aubergine (eggplant) is soft – about 10 minutes over a medium heat.

Pour the contents of the pan into a food processor or liquidiser, with the seasoning and the cumin, and reduce it all to a speckled purée. This can also be done the traditional way with a pestle and mortar.

Serve the purée warm, with chunks of bread for dipping.

Fried green peppers
Pimientos fritos

Mediterranean housewives can choose specially-grown, thin-fleshed green peppers for frying. If you can find them, buy them for this dish. It can be made with the widely available thick-fleshed variety – which in Spain would be used for stuffing or in salads – but they must be cut into strips for frying.

Makes 8 tapa mouthfuls   Serves 2 as a starter   (Pictured on page 71)

| 8 small thin-fleshed green peppers or 2 large thick-fleshed red sweet or green peppers | 4 tablespoons olive oil |
| | salt |

If the peppers are the small thin-fleshed variety, wipe them and leave them whole. If you have the thick-fleshed peppers hull, de-seed and cut them into finger-width (1.5 cm/½-inch) strips.

Heat the oil in a frying pan (skillet) until a faint blue haze rises. Throw in the peppers. Cook them fiercely but briefly, turning until all sides take a little colour. Turn the heat right down and lid the pan. Cook over a gentle heat until the peppers are soft. Add salt to taste.

Take out the peppers and arrange them in a dish. Serve them hot or cold, sauced with their own cooking juices, with plenty of bread to mop up the aromatic oil.

Aubergine (eggplant) fritters
Berejenas fritas

This tapa is quickly prepared and cheap. It's also delicious. What more can anyone ask? The same technique can be applied to courgettes (zucchini). In my family the fritters vanish as soon as they come out of the pan.

Makes 10–12 tapa mouthfuls   Serves 2 as a starter, with a fresh tomato sauce (page 101)   (Pictured on page 126)

1 large aubergine (eggplant)	1 teaspoon paprika
2 tablespoons milk	oil for shallow-frying
2 tablespoons plain (all-purpose) flour	salt

Wipe and hull the aubergine (eggplant) and cut it into thin slices. Salt the slices and put them in a colander to drain for half an hour (I don't always do this, but it is traditional). Rinse and pat dry.

Pour the milk on to a flat plate. Spread the flour on to another plate and mix in the paprika.

Heat a finger's width (1.5 cm/½ inch) of oil in a frying pan (skillet). When it hazes with blue smoke, dip the slices of aubergine (eggplant) first in the milk and then in the flour, and then slip them into the hot oil. Fry them to a crisp. Transfer to kitchen paper to drain.

Continue until all the aubergine (eggplant) is done. Serve the fritters immediately.

Fried baby artichokes
Alcachofitas fritas

A very quick and easy way with the small leaf artichokes, no bigger than a baby's fist, which sometimes come our way at the beginning of the season in May and June. These juniors are sold tied by the stalk, in bundles of six to twelve. Only buy them if they have fresh tight heads like budding flowers. Mature artichokes can be prepared in this way, but the outside and tops of the leaves and the choke must be trimmed off first. This is my favourite tapa.

Makes 24 tapa mouthfuls   Serves 2 as a starter   (Pictured on page 53)

6 baby artichokes
olive oil for shallow-frying
salt

1 lemon, quartered, to
serve

Wipe the artichokes and trim the stalks off level with the base. With a sharp knife, peel off the rough outside of the stalks and cut them in half lengthways – if they are very slender, leave them whole. Quarter the artichokes straight through the base.

Heat two fingers' width (3 cm/1 inch) of oil in a frying pan (skillet). When it hazes faint blue, put in as many quarters of artichoke as the pan will accommodate in one layer. Fry the artichokes until the leaves are crisp and brown and the choke tender. Continue until all are fried, leaving the stalks until the end. Drain on kitchen paper, sprinkle with salt and serve with the quartered lemon. They are to be eaten in the fingers, from the choke towards the leaves, as far as is tender.

Baked peppers and tomatoes
Asadillo

This is served as a tapa in the Venta del Quixote at Puerto Lapis near Aranjuez, La Mancha. It's delicious cold and keeps well in a screw-top jar in the fridge – although it should be brought up to room temperature before serving.

Makes 8–10 tapa mouthfuls   Serves 2 as a starter

2 red sweet peppers
3 tablespoons olive oil
1 garlic clove, chopped
2 tomatoes, sliced

1 teaspoon dried marjoram
or oregano
salt and pepper

Preheat the oven to Gas Mark 8/230°C/450°F.

Using a long toasting fork carefully roast the whole peppers over a gas flame, or under the grill, until the skin blisters black (the kitchen fills with the most delicious aroma). Hull, skin and de-seed the peppers. Cut them into strips.

Oil 4 individual shallow casseroles, or one larger one. Arrange the peppers, garlic and tomato in layers, seasoning as you go. Sprinkle with the rest of the oil and the marjoram or oregano. Bake in the oven for 20–25 minutes.

Serve hot in their dish or dishes, with bread for mopping.

Broad beans with ham
Habas con jamón

Simple and quickly prepared, these quantities make an excellent little supper dish for one. Bacon is a closer approximation to the Spanish wind-dried hams than cooked ham. Any salt-cured raw ham is fine for this dish.

Makes 10–12 tapa mouthfuls   Serves 2 as a starter   (Pictured on page 71)

250 g (8 oz) shelled broad beans (fresh or frozen)
2 tablespoons olive oil
1–2 slices of lean bacon or salt-cured ham, chopped
1 tablespoon chopped parsley
salt and pepper

Blanch the broad beans in boiling, salted water for 2–3 minutes, unless they are old ones in which case they will need 6–10 minutes to become tender.

Warm the oil in a small pan. Add the chopped bacon or ham and fry it for a minute or two. Stir in the parsley and the beans. Lid and cook gently for 5 minutes. Taste and add salt and pepper.

Serve in small individual dishes, or on a single plate with forks for each person.

Asparagus with soft-boiled eggs
Espárragos con huevos

This is a delicious version of nursery eggs. It is nicest made with the slender bright green stalks of sprue – wild-gathered asparagus – in Mediterranean countries. It can be made with the fat cultivated stalks if you prefer.

Makes 12–18 tapa mouthfuls   Serves 4 as a starter   (Pictured on page 90)

500 g (1 lb) asparagus sprue
4 small eggs (size 4)
salt

Wash and trim the asparagus. Tie them in a neat bundle and set them upright in a pan of boiling, salted water, so that the stalks are in water and the tops in steam only. Drain them when tender but not floppy – 5–7 minutes should do.

Soft-boil the eggs – 3–4 minutes, depending on size.

Serve each person with a decapitated egg in an egg-cup, a little salt, and a helping of asparagus for dipping.

Clams in sherry (page 91)
Fried baby artichokes (page 50)
Russian salad with mayonnaise (page 31)
Green beans with spiced almonds (page 60)
Steaks with blue cheese (page 102)
Moorish kebabs (page 114)

New potato salad (page 40)
Baked mushrooms with parsley and garlic (page 48)
Courgettes (zucchini) in tomato sauce (page 62)
Artichokes in oil (page 39)
Aubergine (eggplant) purée (page 48)

Gratin of cardoons or chard stalks
Cardo o acelga gratinado

These two vegetables are particularly popular in winter in Spain, when there is not much else around. Cardoons are a member of the artichoke family, and their flavour is similar. I've had them served plain-boiled, dressed with olive oil and salt and pepper, and sometimes, as here, baked in a white sauce. Be careful, though, as the cardoon is very bitter unless it is properly trimmed of all its leaves. Chard is a good alternative, and easier to come by.

Makes 18–20 tapa mouthfuls   Serves 3–4 as a starter   (Pictured on page 144)

3–4 inner stalks of cardoon or Swiss chard
1 tablespoon lemon juice or wine vinegar
2 tablespoons olive oil
25 g (1 oz) (¼ cup) plain (all-purpose) flour
1 tablespoon dry sherry
350 ml (12 fl oz) (1½ cups) milk or beef or chicken stock
50 g (2 oz) (½ cup) grated hard cheese (Manchego or Cheddar)
salt and pepper

If you are using cardoons, trim off the little fringe of leaf which edges the stalks, and discard the heart – all these are very bitter. If you use Swiss chard, use only the white stalks, and save the green leaves to use in the recipe for vinegar-dressed chard leaves on page 59.

Cut the stalks into bite-sized pieces and rinse them. Bring a pan of salted water to the boil. Add the lemon juice or vinegar and put in the cardoon or chard. Bring back to the boil, lid and cook for 20 minutes, until the stalks are tender. Drain well and arrange in a shallow *gratin* dish.

Meanwhile make a white sauce. Warm the oil in a small pan. Stir in the flour and cook for a moment to mix the two. Add the sherry. Pour in the rest of the liquid gradually, whisking to avoid lumps. Cook gently until the sauce is thick enough to coat the back of the spoon. Beat in half the cheese. Taste and add salt and pepper.

Pour the sauce over and around the cooked vegetables. Sprinkle with the rest of the grated cheese and slide the dish under the grill to melt and brown the cheese.

New potatoes with garlic and saffron
Patatas frescas en ajopollo

The Moors, who colonised Andalucía for five centuries, left their mark on Spanish cuisine. Potatoes are given a Moorish treatment in this dish from Malaga. It makes a delicious first course. The dish can be prepared in advance up to the final reduction of the sauce.

Makes about 8 tapa mouthfuls   Serves 2 as a starter

250 g (8 oz) small new potatoes
2 tablespoons olive oil
1 tablespoon fresh breadcrumbs
1 garlic clove, crushed
6 blanched almonds
1 tablespoon chopped parsley
2–3 saffron threads infused in a little boiling water, or ½ teaspoon saffron powder or tumeric
2 tablespoons water
salt and pepper

Scrub the potatoes well but leave them whole.

Heat the oil in a small frying pan (skillet). Fry the breadcrumbs, garlic and almonds in the oil until all are lightly golden. Tip the contents of the pan, with the parsley and saffron or turmeric and water, into a food processor. Process until the mixture is a thick paste. You can do this with a pestle and mortar if you prefer.

Put the potatoes into a small saucepan. Add enough water to just submerge the potatoes. Tip in the paste. Bring to the boil, lid and cook gently until the potatoes are tender – about 15 minutes. Take off the lid and boil rapidly until the sauce is well reduced. Taste and add salt and pepper.

Serve the potatoes hot or cold, in their sauce.

French fries
Patatas fritas

This is the easiest and most delicious of tapas – well worth making your own with olive oil. It knocks spots off oven french fries. Children will always eat french fries, even if everything else looks strange to them. The triple-cooking ensures crispness.

Makes 30–40 french fries   (Pictured on page 143)

3–4 large old potatoes	salt
olive oil for frying (about	
600 ml/1 pint/2½ cups	
re-usable)	

Wash, peel and slice the potatoes. Cut them into chips about the length and width of an index finger.

Heat the oil in a small enough pan to give you a depth of about two fingers (3 cm/1 inch). When it is lightly hazed with blue, put in as many of the french fries as the pan will accommodate easily.

Bring the oil back to the boil, turn down the heat and cook the french fries gently until they are tender but have not taken colour. Transfer them to a colander to drain the excess oil into a bowl. Continue with the rest of the potato.

Pour the excess oil back into the pan and reheat until the blue haze rises again. Re-fry the french fries until pale gold and beginning to crisp. Remove as before and drain.

Repeat the previous exercise when you are ready to serve the french fries. This time make sure the oil is very hot. The french fries will gild and crisp immediately.

Sprinkle them with salt and eat them scalding hot.

Re-fried cauliflower with garlic
Coliflor al ajo arriero

This dish is a great weakness of mine – the quantity makes a delicious supper for one. It's just as good cold as hot.

Makes 15–18 tapa mouthfuls   Serves 2 as a starter

1 small cauliflower	1 tablespoon sherry or
3–4 tablespoons olive oil	wine vinegar
1–2 garlic cloves, chopped	salt and pepper
1 teaspoon paprika	
1 tablespoon chopped	
parsley	

Wash the cauliflower and divide it into bite-sized florets. Cook it in boiling, salted water until soft. Drain.

Heat the oil in a frying pan (skillet). Turn the garlic in the hot oil until it softens and takes a little colour. Throw in the paprika and add the cauliflorets. Fry for a few minutes until the cauliflower browns a little. Sprinkle on the parsley, vinegar and salt and pepper.

Serve hot or cold, with forks for everyone.

Potatoes with pepper and tomato sauce
Machacón

This cheap-and-cheerful dish from La Mancha is made with baked potatoes in the winter – and the winters in La Mancha are harsh. Make it at the same time as the recipe for new potatoes on page 56 for a pretty contrast.

Makes 8–10 tapa mouthfuls   Serves 2 as a starter

250 g (8 oz) small new
  potatoes
1 tablespoon chopped
  green pepper
1 large tomato, skinned
  and chopped
1 tablespoon chopped
  cucumber

2 tablespoons lemon juice
2–3 tablespoons olive oil
1 teaspoon cumin seeds,
  dry-roasted and crushed
  (optional)
salt and pepper

Scrub and cook the new potatoes in boiling, salted water until soft – about 15 minutes, depending on size. Drain them thoroughly.

Mix the chopped vegetables with the lemon juice and oil, and salt and pepper to taste.

Shake the hot potatoes so they split a little. Dress them with the sauce and the roasted cumin seeds, if used.

Serve hot, either on individual saucers or a single plate, with a fork for each guest.

Peppery potatoes
Patatas bravas

This deliciously simple hot tapa is served in a back-street bar in Granada. The cheaper establishments in Spain are very inventive with potatoes.

Makes 10–12 tapa mouthfuls   Serves 2 as a starter   (Pictured on page 90)

2 large old potatoes
4 tablespoons olive oil
1 teaspoon paprika

¼ teaspoon cayenne
  pepper
salt

Preheat the oven to Gas Mark 8/230°C/450°F. Alternatively, the cooking can be done on the top of the cooker – either in a heavy frying pan (skillet), or in a casserole which will resist direct heat.

Peel the potatoes and cut them into thick wedges. Pour half the oil into 4 individual shallow earthenware casseroles or a small *gratin* dish.

Put the casseroles or the dish into the oven and leave until the oil is smoking.

Arrange the potatoes in the hot oil in a single layer. Trickle on the rest of the oil, sprinkle with salt and return to the oven. Cook the potatoes until soft inside and crisp on the outside – this will take 25–35 minutes.

Mix together the paprika and cayenne and sprinkle over the potatoes. Serve them hot in their cooking dish.

Spinach or chard leaves dressed with vinegar
Espinacas o acelgas con vinagre

I had this delicious little dish in a *venta* (small country bar) in Baeza. It makes a very good first course for four if you double the quantities. Combine it with the recipe using chard stalks on page 55 if you are using chard.

Makes 10 tapa mouthfuls   Serves 2 as a starter   (Pictured on page 125)

250 g (8 oz) leaf spinach (fresh or frozen) or green chard leaves	4 tablespoons olive oil
1 tablespoon fresh breadcrumbs	1 teaspoon sherry or wine vinegar
	salt and pepper

Rinse, pick over, shred and cook the fresh leaves in a lidded pan with a little salt and the minimum of water. This will take about 5 minutes only. Frozen leaf spinach must be defrosted first.

Meanwhile, fry the breadcrumbs golden in the olive oil.

When the spinach is cooked, drain it well and turn it in the hot oil. Finish with a sprinkle of vinegar, pepper and breadcrumbs.

Pile it on a single pretty white plate, or in 4 little dishes to serve 4 as a tapa.

Green beans with spiced almonds
Judías verdes con almendras

This dish originates in Valencia, where five centuries ago the Moors planted almond groves for their favourite honey and almond *halva*. The modern *turrón* (nougat) industry springs from these roots.

Makes 12–15 tapa mouthfuls   *Serves 2 as a starter*   (*Pictured on page 53*)

250g (8oz) green beans, de-stringed and cut into short lengths
25g (1oz) (¼ cup) flaked almonds
2 tablespoons olive oil
1 teaspoon paprika
juice of ½ lemon
salt

Bring a pan of salted water to the boil and throw in the beans. Cook them until tender but still green and firm – 4–6 minutes.

Meanwhile cut the flaked almonds into matchsticks. Heat the olive oil in a small frying pan (skillet) and fry the almonds golden – a few seconds only or you will burn both nuts and oil. Stir in the paprika off the heat.

Drain the beans and toss them with the lemon juice and the contents of the frying pan. Taste and add salt if necessary.

Serve on a plate, with forks for each tapa eater.

Tomatoes stuffed with pine kernels
Tomates rellenos con piñones

Bite-sized tomatoes are perfect as tapas. For a first course for four, use large beef tomatoes and double the stuffing quantities.

Makes 8 tapa mouthfuls   *Serves 2 as a starter*   (*Pictured on page 89*)

8 small tomatoes
3 tablespoons olive oil
1 tablespoon pine kernels or flaked almonds
1 tablespoon chopped onion
1 garlic clove, chopped
1 tablespoon chopped parsley
4 tablespoons fresh breadcrumbs
salt and pepper

Preheat the oven to Gas Mark 7/220°C/425°F.

Wipe each tomato and slice off a small lid. Take out the

seeds and discard them. Scoop out the centre flesh and reserve it along with the tomato lids.

Warm 2 tablespoons of the oil in a small pan and add the pine kernels or almonds. Let them take colour; then remove and drain. Lightly fry the onion and garlic. Tip in the reserved tomato flesh and allow the mixture to bubble up into a little sauce. Stir in the herbs, breadcrumbs and fried nuts. Taste and add salt and pepper.

Arrange the hollow tomatoes in an oiled baking dish. Stuff them with the breadcrumb mixture. Trickle over the rest of the oil and bake in the oven for 20–30 minutes until well-browned.

Serve the little tomatoes whole in their cooking dish, with forks or cocktail sticks for easy handling.

Peppers stuffed with rice and mushrooms
Pimientos rellenos con arroz y setas

This is a speciality of José Luis Gregorio, the chef at the old Venta del Pilar just outside Alcoy in the hills behind Valencia. He serves the stuffed peppers hot in winter – it's cold in those shepherding uplands; in the summer they're just as good cold.

Makes 24–30 tapa mouthfuls   Serves 4 as a starter

4 large red sweet or green peppers
2 tablespoons olive oil
2 garlic cloves, chopped
2–3 mushrooms, chopped
50 g (2 oz) lean bacon or salt-cured ham, chopped
1 tablespoon paprika
1 tablespoon chopped parsley
500 g (1 lb) tomatoes, skinned and chopped
1 wine glass of water
250 g (8 oz) (1 cup) round pudding rice
½ teaspoon salt
4 saffron threads infused in 1 tablespoon hot water and crushed, or ½ teaspoon turmeric

Preheat the oven to Gas Mark 7/220°C/425°F.

Wipe the peppers and cut off a lid round the stalk end, leaving the stalk in place. Empty out the seeds.

Make a *sofrito*: heat the oil gently in a frying pan (skillet). Throw in the garlic and let it soften for a few moments. Add the mushrooms and bacon or ham and fry for a few more minutes. Stir in the paprika, parsley, tomatoes and water.

Let the mixture bubble up. Stir in the rice, salt and saffron or turmeric and remove from the heat.

Use the rice mixture to stuff the peppers – only half full as the rice needs room to swell. Arrange the peppers upright, mouths pointing heavenwards, in a pan which will just accommodate them. Replace their lids.

Cover and cook in the oven for about 1¼ hours. Test after 1 hour, by biting a grain of rice: the rice on top will be very soft if the middle is properly cooked.

Serve the peppers hot or cold, neatly cut into bite-sized portions in their cooking dish, with forks. If serving the peppers as a starter, allow one whole one for each person.

Courgettes (zucchini) in tomato sauce
Calabacines a la riojana

This is an aromatic vegetable stew from Don Quixote's home territory. Any vegetable – potatoes, beans, aubergines (eggplants), carrots – will respond happily to similar treatment.

Makes 18–20 tapa mouthfuls   Serves 3–4 as a starter   (Pictured on page 54)

2–3 tablespoons olive oil
4–5 courgettes (zucchini), sliced into bite-sized rings
2 garlic cloves, chopped
1 medium-size onion, chopped
250 g (8 oz) tomatoes, skinned and chopped (fresh or canned)

½ teaspoon thyme
1 bay leaf
1 wine glass of water
1 tablespoon chopped parsley
salt and pepper

Heat the olive oil in a saucepan. Throw in the courgettes (zucchini) and fry them for 2–3 minutes. Remove and reserve. Add the garlic and onion to the pan and let them fry gently until they soften but do not take colour.

Add the chopped tomatoes, thyme and bay leaf; bubble up, mash lightly and let all simmer for a minute or two to a thick purée.

Return the courgettes (zucchini) to the pan. Pour in the water and bring all to the boil. Turn down the heat, lid and leave to simmer for 6–8 minutes, until the courgettes (zucchini) are tender but still bright green. If the sauce is too sloppy, boil it up fiercely for a moment or two. Taste and add salt and pepper. Stir in the parsley.

This dish is just as good hot or cold. Serve it in a shallow earth-brown earthenware casserole.

Vegetables with oil-and-garlic
Hervido con all-i-oli

This is Valencia's favourite sauce accompanied by the products of her excellent market gardens. In summer, serve the garlic sauce with raw fresh vegetables.

Makes 20–24 tapa mouthfuls Serves 3–4 as a starter

1 large carrot, cut into bite-sized lengths
1 large potato, peeled and cubed
1 turnip, cubed
½ small cauliflower, divided into florets
a handful of green beans, topped and tailed

salt

GARLIC SAUCE
3 garlic cloves
½ teaspoon salt
about 150 ml (¼ pint) (⅔ cup) olive oil

Bring a pan of salted water to the boil. If you have a good home-made stock – maybe from boiled beef, bacon or chicken – use that instead. Add the vegetables to the boiling liquid in the order listed, bringing it back to the boil each time. The operation will take about 20 minutes.

While the vegetables cook, settle down with a pestle and mortar to make the *all-i-oli* (garlic-and-oil) – a soothing process.

Chop the garlic roughly and crush it in the mortar with the salt. When the garlic is well pounded, start adding the oil in a thin stream. Keep pounding with the pestle and trickling in the oil until the mixture is good and thick.

Serve in its mortar or a small bowl, alongside the boiled vegetables for dipping.

Note: if you are in a hurry, make the sauce in a food processor or liquidiser, with a slice of boiled potato, or a crust of stale bread, soaked and squeezed, to stabilise it. Those uncertain of good results can make it with an egg yolk – like garlic mayonnaise – which gives a richer but less piquant mix.

Whole broad bean casserole
Habas a la rondeña

This slow-cooked stew, aromatic with wine and herbs, is my favourite vegetable dish. I first tasted it in its home-territory, the fortified hill-town of Ronda. The evening air is always cool in these mountains, even in summer, and many of the local dishes were traditionally simmered over a shallow brazier which used to do duty as central heating under the table. Double the quantities and finish with quarters of hard-boiled eggs for a perfect summer lunch for two.

Makes 15–20 tapa mouthfuls   Serves 2 as a starter

500 g (1 lb) young broad beans in their pods
3 tablespoons olive oil
1 small onion, chopped
1 garlic clove, chopped
50 g (2 oz) lean bacon or salt-cured ham, chopped
1 small glass of dry sherry
1 large glass of water
1 tablespoon fresh breadcrumbs
1 tablespoon chopped parsley
salt and pepper

Top, tail and string the young beans in their pods; then chop them into short lengths, more or less following the swell of each bean. Do not do this in advance as the beans are inclined to turn navy blue at the edges. Podded beans can be used without further attention.

Warm the oil in a casserole or heavy pan. Fry the onion and garlic for a moment without allowing them to take colour. Add the chopped bacon or ham, and then the beans.

Pour in the sherry and water, add salt and pepper, and bring all to the boil. Cover and stew gently for 1½ hours (this can also be done in a gentle oven at Gas Mark 3/160°C/ 325°F.) Check intermittently and add more water if necessary. When the beans are tender, bubble up uncovered for a moment to evaporate the liquid – it should be juicy but not swimming.

Stir in the breadcrumbs and the parsley. Reheat, taste and add more salt and pepper if necessary.

Serve either in tapa portions in saucers, or in a pretty earthenware dish for sharing. Accompany with chunks of good bread to mop up the juices.

Eggs and tortillas

Eggs are the staple of the Spanish larder – as befits a rural economy with a strong peasant-farming tradition. The egg-lady, the *recovrera*, still, in the 1970s, collected surplus eggs from our neighbours in the remote Andalucían valley in which we lived. She would take the eggs to sell in the local market in Algeciras. Her suppliers would receive their payment in kind: salt and sugar, condensed milk and coffee – all items which could not be home-grown or made.

Any Spanish housewife who can wield more than a can-opener turns out a perfect Spanish omelette, the *tortilla española*. This is a thick, juicy egg-and-potato cake which bears only a passing resemblance to its frothy French cousin. There is a wide repertoire of these egg-cakes with many regional variations – visitors to Valencia will find a tapa bar serving nothing but different varieties of tortilla, dozens of them.

Eggs are often served fried, either on the griddle plate (*a la plancha*) in shallow oil in a pan (*frito*), or casserole-fried in a shallow earthenware dish over direct heat (*al plato*). Otherwise, they are hard-boiled and served in salads, or sometimes chopped and added to a stew or soup to compensate for a shortage of meat. They are also, of course, the foundation for the ever-popular mayonnaise. In the north, they may come scrambled with vegetables as the Basque national dish, *piparrada*.

In Britain there has been a scare recently about eggs and salmonella, although I haven't come across it myself. But if you are worried about any dishes that contain raw or lightly cooked eggs, you might want to consult your egg supplier first or avoid them altogether, particularly if you are in a high risk group.

Spanish potato omelette
Tortilla española

The potato tortilla is not only the mainstay of the tapa table, it is staple picnic-fare all over Spain, and the nearest thing to a national dish. Children take it to school for lunch; grannies thrive on it; every household has its own special way of making it, the person who makes it best, and the perfect pan to cook it in. Garlic and parsley are sometimes included, but I like the clean fresh flavour of this simple recipe.

Makes 20–24 bite-sized cubes   Serves 4 as a starter   (Pictured on page 89)

750 g (1½ lb) potatoes
(allow 1 large potato per egg)
4 tablespoons olive oil
1 thick slice of Spanish (mild) onion, chopped finely

3 eggs
½ teaspoon salt

Peel and cut the potatoes into thin slices or fat french fries. Put the oil to heat in a small omelette pan. Fry the potatoes and the onion gently in the oil. Cook the potatoes until they are quite soft, but have not taken colour.

Transfer the potato and onion to a sieve placed over a bowl to catch the oil as it drains.

Beat the eggs lightly with the salt. Add the drained potatoes. Pour most of the oil out of the pan, leaving only a tablespoon or two. Return the pan to the heat and tip in the egg-potato mixture. The heat should be low or the base will burn before the eggs are ready. With a spatula, push the potato down into the egg so that all is submerged.

As the tortilla cooks, neaten the sides with a metal spatula to build up a deep, straight edge. When it looks firm, slide it out on to a plate; then invert it back into the pan to cook the other side. A little more oil in the pan may be necessary. Don't overcook the tortilla – the centre should remain juicy. When the tortilla feels lightly set and firm, remove it and drain it well on kitchen paper.

Serve the tortilla warm or cold, cut into bite-sized cubes, each pierced with a cocktail stick.

Sacro-Monte omelette
Tortilla al Sacro-Monte

This is a celebrated tortilla from Granada – a speciality of the Sacro-Monte, the cave-dwelling gypsy quarter in the cliffs above the Alhambra. It is essentially a dish of the urban poor. The variety meats which the city's wealthy burgers did not want were cheap and easily available to the less well-off citizens. The rich were missing a treat.

Makes 20–24 bite-sized cubes   Serves 2 as a main course

1 pig's or lamb's brain
2–3 sweetbreads
3–4 tablespoons olive oil
1 large potato, peeled and cubed small (optional)
2 lamb's kidneys, skinned, cored and sliced thinly
50 g (2 oz) salt-cured ham or lean bacon, chopped finely

1 tablespoon chopped red sweet pepper
1 tablespoon shelled peas (fresh or frozen)
4 eggs
salt and pepper

Simmer the brain and sweetbreads in enough lightly salted water to cover. When they are firm and cooked through – about 20 minutes – drain and leave to cool, weighted between two plates to allow them to firm. Skin and slice them.

Meanwhile heat the oil in a small omelette pan. Add the potato cubes (if you have plenty of brains and sweetbreads, the potato can be omitted). Cook the potato until soft, but do not let the temperature rise so that it takes colour. Transfer the potato to a sieve over a small basin to catch the drips of extra oil.

Fry the sliced brain and sweetbreads to brown them a little. Transfer to the sieve. Do the same for the kidney, ham or bacon, and chopped red sweet pepper. Turn the peas in the oil last.

Beat the eggs lightly with salt and pepper. Mix in the cooked ingredients.

Return the oil drippings to the pan and reheat. Tip in the egg mixture, and cook it in a thick pancake, following the instructions opposite.

Serve warm or cool, cut into bite-sized cubes and speared with cocktail sticks.

Country omelette
Tortilla a la payesa

This is a fine solid omelette, a meal in itself, and excellent for a winter picnic. It is made all over Spain, using various local sausages and seasonal vegetables.

Makes 20–24 bite-sized cubes   Serves 2 as a main course

4–5 tablespoons olive oil
1 large potato, peeled and sliced finely
50 g (2 oz) salt-cured ham or lean bacon, diced
1 garlic clove, chopped
1 slice of onion, chopped
1 small tomato, chopped
125 g (4 oz) green beans, top-and-tailed and chopped into short lengths
4 tablespoons shelled peas (fresh or frozen)
4 eggs
salt and pepper

Heat 3 tablespoons of the oil in an omelette pan. Add the sliced potatoes and cook them gently until tender. Remove and drain in a sieve over a bowl to catch the drippings.

Reheat the oil. Throw in the ham or bacon, garlic and onion. Fry gently until all soften and take colour. Add the tomato, beans and peas and bubble up to evaporate any extra liquid.

Beat the eggs lightly with salt and pepper and mix in the cooked ingredients, including the contents of the pan.

Add the rest of the oil, including the drippings, to the pan. Tip in the egg mixture and cook as a thick pancake, following the instructions on page 66.

Serve warm or cool, cut into neat bite-sized cubes and speared with cocktail sticks.

Beans and sausage omelette
Tortilla catalana

This is a popular tapa omelette in the bars of Barcelona, capital of Cataluna and Spain's second city. The sausage used is butifarra, the Catalan's version of the southerners' chorizo. Butifarra is spiced with cinnamon, cloves and nutmeg rather than paprika. Chick-peas and salami with spices can replace the beans and butifarra in the recipe.

Makes 15–20 bite-sized cubes   Serves 2 as a main course

2 tablespoons olive oil
2 tablespoons cubed
  butifarra, or salami with
  1 teaspoon mixed spice
250 g (8 oz) cooked haricot
  or butter beans (fresh or
  canned)

3 eggs
salt and pepper

Warm a tablespoon of the olive oil in an omelette pan. Fry the sausage for a few minutes until the edges brown and the fat runs. Stir in the spices if using the salami. Add the well-drained beans and warm them through.

Beat the eggs lightly with salt and pepper and mix in the contents of the pan.

Wipe the pan and then heat the rest of the oil. Tip in the egg mixture and cook as a thick pancake, following the instructions on page 66.

Serve warm or cool, cut into neat bite-sized cubes and speared with cocktail sticks.

Spinach omelette
Tortilla de espinacas

This Valencian tortilla makes an excellent fresh-flavoured tapa. It's one of my own favourites for a light summer lunch.

Makes 12–15 bite-sized cubes   Serves 2 as a main course

500 g (1 lb) leaf spinach
  (fresh or frozen)
4 eggs
1 tablespoon toasted pine
  kernels or slivered
  almonds (optional)

2 tablespoons olive oil
salt and pepper

Wash the spinach if it's fresh. Remove any tough stalks and shred the leaves. Blanch the spinach in the water which clings to it. Drain as soon as it goes limp, and press it dry in a sieve. Leave to cool a little.

Lightly beat the eggs with salt and pepper. Stir in the spinach and the nuts if you are using them.

Heat the oil in a small omelette pan. Tip in the egg mixture. Cook as a thick pancake, following the instructions on page 66.

Serve warm or cool, cut into bite-sized cubes and speared with cocktail sticks.

Omelette in spiced parsley sauce
Tortilla en salsa de Clavijo

This tortilla is a speciality of Clavijo near Logroño. Clavijo is the site of the famous Moorish–Christian battle of AD 844, in which St James the Apostle miraculously intervened on the side of the angels, inspiring the legend of the Matamoro – Santiago de Compostela.

The tortilla can be made ahead and reheated in the Moorish-spiced sauce.

Makes 16–20 bite-sized cubes   Serves 4 as a starter

THE OMELETTE
4 tablespoons fresh
    breadcrumbs
6 tablespoons milk
4 eggs
2 tablespoons olive oil
salt and pepper

THE SAUCE
2 tablespoons olive oil

1 tablespoon plain (all-
    purpose) flour
¼ teaspoon ground cloves
½ teaspoon ground
    cinnamon
200 ml (7 fl oz) (¾ cup)
    milk or chicken stock
1 tablespoon chopped
    parsley
salt and pepper

Put the breadcrumbs to soak with the milk for 10 minutes.

Fork the eggs lightly with salt and pepper. Mix the breadcrumbs into the egg.

Heat the oil in a small omelette pan – it should be good and hot. Pour in the egg mixture. Lid and cook gently until the egg is set. Slide it out on to a plate, reheat the pan and add extra oil if necessary. Reverse the omelette back into the pan and cook the other side. Remove and cut, when cool, into bite-sized squares.

Meanwhile make the sauce. Warm the oil in a small saucepan. Sprinkle in the flour and cook until sandy – don't let it brown. Add the spices and then whisk in the milk or stock. Bring to the boil and then simmer gently, whisking as it thickens. Stir in the parsley. Taste and add salt and pepper.

Reheat the tortilla pieces in the sauce. Serve hot, speared with cocktail sticks.

Fried green peppers (page 49)
Broad beans with ham (page 52)
Pork medallions with lemon and marjoram (page 105)
Potato mayonnaise with red sweet peppers (page 32)
Griddled tuna or swordfish steaks (page 80)

Tomatoes with garlic and marjoram (page 44)
Whelks with spiced vinegar (page 92)
Monkfish kebabs (page 84)
Salad kebabs (page 42)
Seafood salad (page 44)

Artichoke omelette
Tortilla de alcachofas

Artichokes, the wild version of which grow all over Spain, are a good partner to pale dry fino sherry such as La Ina. They do delicious things to the taste of the wine.

Makes 15–20 bite-sized cubes   Serves 2 as a main course

4 medium-size artichokes (or canned artichoke hearts)	50 g (2 oz) salt-cured ham or lean bacon, diced
4 tablespoons olive oil	4 eggs
	salt and pepper

Remove the hard outside leaves and trim the base of the artichokes. Trim off the points of the leaves close to the choke, leaving only as much as looks tender and pale. With a sharp knife, nick out and discard the hairy central choke. This will leave just the heart. Slice it thinly.

Warm the oil in a small omelette pan, and throw in the slices of artichoke. Fry gently until soft and lightly browned. Half-way through, add the diced ham or bacon.

Remove and transfer to a sieve over a small basin to catch the drippings.

Beat the eggs lightly together with salt and pepper. Stir in the cooled artichokes and ham or bacon.

Reheat the oil, together with the drippings from the basin. Tip in the egg mixture. Cook as a thick pancake, following the instructions on page 66.

Serve warm or cool, cut into bite-sized cubes and speared with cocktail sticks.

Asparagus sprue omelette
Tortilla de espárragos trigueras

This is a favourite springtime tapa throughout Andalucía, where gypsies sell small bundles of wild asparagus in the markets. Bitter and sweet varieties are usually on offer, and the best mix is a few of the first and a lot of the second. The fine green stalks of cultivated asparagus – sprue – are perfect for this dish. Big fat white ones can be used – they should be trimmed and sliced very finely.

Makes 15–20 bite-sized cubes   Serves 3–4 as a starter

> 500 g (1 lb) thin green
>   asparagus sprue
> 2 tablespoons olive oil
>
> 3 eggs
> salt and pepper

Snap off the hard woody ends of the asparagus and discard. Chop the rest of the stalks into pea-sized lengths.

Warm a tablespoon of the olive oil in an omelette pan. Turn the asparagus in the hot oil for a moment or two until it turns bright green and softens a little. Drain in a colander over a bowl for the oil drippings.

Beat the eggs lightly with salt and pepper and mix in the asparagus.

Reheat all the oil, including the drippings. Tip in the egg mixture and cook as a thick pancake, following the instructions on page 66.

Serve warm or cool, cut into neat bite-sized cubes and speared with cocktail sticks.

Mushroom and garlic omelette
Tortilla de setas y ajos frescos

This is a popular summertime tapa in Valencia, where it is made with wild-gathered orange milk caps (*lactaria deliciosa*) and fresh garlic. These last look like white onions and have a mild flavour since they are used before the cloves have had time to form. Wild garlic grows throughout Europe, and many countries, including Britain, have similar recipes. I give here a combination of garlic cloves and spring onions as a replacement for hard-to-find fresh garlic, and button mushrooms to replace the orange milk caps.

Makes 15–20 bite-sized cubes   Serves 2 as a main course

375 g (12 oz) button mushrooms	2 large spring onions (white part only), sliced
4 tablespoons olive oil	4 eggs
2 garlic cloves, sliced	salt and pepper

Wipe (don't rinse) and slice the mushrooms. Heat the oil in a small omelette pan. Add the mushrooms. Cook them gently until all their moisture has evaporated and the oil is clear again.

Remove and drain in a sieve over a bowl to catch the drippings.

Add the garlic and sliced spring onions to the remaining oil in the pan. Fry them gently until they soften. Add them to the mushrooms in the sieve.

Beat the eggs lightly with salt and pepper. Stir in the now-cooled vegetables.

Add the oil drippings to the oil in the pan. Reheat and tip in the egg mixture. Cook as a thick pancake, following the instructions on page 66.

Serve warm or cool, cut into bite-sized cubes and speared with cocktail sticks.

Fried quail's eggs
Huevos de codorniz a la plancha

Happily for the population of small wild birds, quail-farming has recently caught on in Spain. I first had these eggs fried on a hot griddle (Spanish cookers have one automatically built in) in a tapa bar in a village in the hills behind Ronda. The little eggs make perfect bite-sized tapas – they are much smaller than hen's eggs, and keep their shape when cooked.

Makes 6 tapa mouthfuls   Serves 2–3 as a starter   (Pictured on page 143)

6 quail's eggs	salt and pepper
1 tablespoon olive oil	
6 small round slices of fresh bread or toast	

Fry the eggs on a very hot griddle or heavy frying pan (skillet) slicked with the olive oil.

Slip each egg on to its round of bread or toast and sprinkle with salt and pepper. That's all. Miniature perfection!

Broad bean omelette
Tortilla de habas

The broad bean was the mainstay of the Spanish diet until Christopher Columbus brought back the haricot bean from the Americas. Spain's wide repertoire of bean-and-pork dishes were all originally based on the broad bean, which could be dried and stored. This recipe uses fresh beans; at the beginning of the season when the beans are young and tiny, use them whole – the pods have a delicate asparagus-like flavour.

Makes 15–20 bite-sized cubes   Serves 2 as a main course

2 tablespoons olive oil
500 g (1 lb) broad beans
    (podded mature beans
    or de-stringed and diced
    young pods)

½ wine glass of sherry
4 eggs
salt and pepper

Warm a tablespoon of the olive oil in an omelette pan. Turn the beans in the hot oil for a moment and then pour in the sherry. Lid the pan and leave the beans to simmer gently for 10–15 minutes, until they are soft. Take off the lid and bubble up at the end to evaporate extra moisture.

Fork up the eggs lightly with salt and pepper and mix in the contents of the pan.

Heat the rest of the oil in the omelette pan. Tip in the egg mixture and cook as a thick pancake, following the instructions on page 66.

Serve warm or cool, cut into neat bite-sized cubes and speared with cocktail sticks.

Scrambled eggs with vegetables
Piparrada

A deliciously juicy combination of eggs and vegetables, this Basque speciality is one of the world's great dishes. It makes a very fine tapa, or the quantities given will make a light lunch for two. The vegetables can be prepared ahead, and the eggs scrambled in at the last minute. Aubergines (eggplants) and courgettes (zucchini) are sometimes among the diced vegetables used.

Makes 12–15 tapa mouthfuls   Serves 4 as a starter

2 tablespoons olive oil
1 garlic clove, chopped
  finely
2 tablespoons finely
  chopped onion
2 tablespoons chopped
  green pepper

2 tablespoons chopped red
  sweet pepper
1 tomato, chopped
2 eggs, beaten lightly
12–15 small squares of
  bread, fried in olive oil
salt and pepper

Heat the oil in a small frying pan (skillet). Turn the garlic, onion and peppers in the hot oil until they soften and take colour. Add the tomato and bubble up to make a thick sauce.

Stir in the beaten eggs and scramble them with the vegetables. Remove from the heat as soon as they set. Season with salt and pepper.

Spoon the eggs on to the squares of fried bread. Serve speared with cocktail sticks.

Scrambled eggs with bacon and spiced sausage
Duelos y quebrantos

This dish of eggs scrambled with ham and spicy chorizo was Don Quixote's treat on a Saturday night. The name literally means wounds-and-suffering – perhaps because the paprika from the sausage bleeds into the eggs. It remains a standard dish in La Mancha, and makes a delicious little hot tapa.

Makes 8–10 tapa mouthfuls   Serves 2 as a starter

2 tablespoons diced salt-
  cured ham or lean bacon
2 tablespoons diced
  chorizo, or salami with
  ½ teaspoon paprika

1 tablespoon olive oil
2 eggs
salt and pepper
squares of bread, to serve

Fry the ham or bacon and the diced sausage in the oil in a small frying pan (skillet). Cook until the meat browns a little and the fat runs. Stir in the paprika if you are using salami.

Meanwhile, lightly fork up the eggs with a little salt and pepper. Add the eggs to the contents of the pan. Turn up the heat. Turn the mixture so that the eggs scramble. As soon as they begin to set, remove the pan from the heat.

Serve on bite-sized squares of bread, each speared with a cocktail stick.

Mixed vegetable omelette
Tortilla murciana

This is a delicious omelette from the fertile market gardens of Murcia, a handsome city founded by the Moors. Any combination of vegetables is good: the proportion of vegetable to egg should remain roughly the same.

Makes 20–24 bite-sized cubes   Serves 2 as a main course

4–5 tablespoons olive oil
1–2 carrots, diced small
125 g (4 oz) green beans, top-and-tailed and chopped into short lengths
125 g (4 oz) courgettes (zucchini), sliced thinly
4 tablespoons shelled peas (fresh or frozen)
50 g (2 oz) salt-cured ham or lean bacon, diced small
1 garlic clove, chopped
1 green pepper, hulled, de-seeded and diced small
3 eggs
salt and pepper

Heat 3 tablespoons of the oil in an omelette pan. Add the carrots, beans, courgettes (zucchini) and peas in sequence, turning them in the hot oil for 3–4 minutes. Remove and drain in a sieve over a bowl to catch the drippings.

Throw in the ham or bacon, garlic and diced green pepper. Fry gently for 2–3 minutes. Remove and drain with the other vegetables.

Beat the eggs lightly with salt and pepper. Stir in the cooked ingredients.

Heat the rest of the oil, plus the drippings, in the omelette pan. Tip in the egg mixture and cook in a thick pancake, following the instructions on page 66.

Serve warm or cool, cut into bite-sized cubes and speared with cocktail sticks.

Flor, a film of living yeast cells, is an extraordinary natural occurrence which ultimately sets apart a fino, such as La Ina, from all other sherries. A freshly opened bottle of La Ina reveals the full aroma of the flor.

Fish, prawns, shrimps and shellfish

Spain harvests magnificent seafood from its surrounding coasts. Most of this bounty from both Atlantic and Mediterranean waters is marketed fresh and unprocessed, trucked through the night to ensure that the inland cities like Madrid get their fish as soon as possible after it is caught. So wide is the variety that the vocabulary to describe the different sea-creatures changes from coast to coast, and even from port to port. When choosing in a bar, the eye and the finger are often the only communication possible to all but the native-born. To make this easy, sea-delicacies are usually laid out for the customers' inspection on a cold counter, priced by weight, and cooked fresh to order.

Prawns and the larger crustaceans are a luxury, with prices to match. So they do not usually appear as a free tapa, but as an individually priced *ración* or portion. Less familiar sea-creatures include sea-tomatoes, sea-lemons, sea-dates, sea-urchins, spiky-shelled sea snails, and a wide variety of shore-crabs. Most esteemed of all is the *percebe* or goose-necked barnacle, a lobster-fleshed sea-creature which looks like a bunch of miniature elephants' feet. Add to that a basketful of the more familiar bi-valves, such as mussels, oysters, clams, razor-shells, scallops and cockles, and it is easy to see why so many Spanish tapa bars specialise in seafood.

The housewives of Andalucía have the lightest hand with the fish frying pan (skillet) – it's said that if they could capture the sea-foam, they'd even fry that to perfection. The whole catch goes into the smoking oil, from sea-anemones to the pin-head-small *chunquetes* (now forbidden fruit); from the tiny jumping shrimps of Cádiz, to steaks cut from the great tuna caught on migration through the Straits of Gibraltar.

Breadcrumbed marinated fish
Pescado en adobo rebozado

This recipe comes from a bar in the old Jewish quarter of Seville; the bar's main house-speciality is Manchego cheese matured in olive oil.

The marination in lemon and garlic adds a Mediterranean flavour to plain white fish.

Makes 16 tapa mouthfuls   Serves 2 as a light main course

8 thin-cut firm white fish steaks weighing about 25–50 g (1–2 oz) each (swordfish, monkfish, tuna, cod or haddock)
juice of 1 lemon
1 garlic clove, chopped

1 egg, beaten with 1 tablespoon milk
3–4 tablespoons fine toasted breadcrumbs
oil for frying (olive and sunflower is a good mix)
salt and pepper

Put the fish steaks to marinate for an hour or two in the lemon juice, garlic and salt and pepper. Remove them and drain well. Dip the steaks in the beaten egg; then coat them firmly with the breadcrumbs.

Heat the oil until it is lightly hazed with blue. Fry the steaks, 2 to 3 at a time so that the oil temperature does not cool too much. Drain on kitchen paper.

Serve hot, with cocktail sticks for easy handling.

Griddled tuna or swordfish steaks
Atún o pez espada a la plancha

Both swordfish and fresh tuna are popular in Spain. They are widely available inland, since their great size makes them ideal for transportation. They are treated more like steak than fish, and are often served as the main course in a meal.

Makes 16 tapa mouthfuls   Serves 4 as a starter   (Pictured on page 71)

8 thin-cut tuna or swordfish steaks weighing about 25 g (1 oz) each
1 tablespoon olive oil

2–3 cos lettuce leaves, shredded
salt and pepper
1 lemon, quartered, to serve

Put the fish to soak for 30 minutes in cold salted water to

drain out any blood. Drain and pat dry. Rub the cut surfaces with the oil and sprinkle with salt and pepper.

Heat a griddle or heavy iron frying pan (skillet) until it is smoking hot. Smack on the steaks. Griddle them fast for 2–3 minutes a side, turning once.

Divide into bite-sized pieces, and spear each piece with a cocktail stick on a small bit of the lettuce leaf. Serve with lemon quarters.

Fried fish
Pescado frito

Each port has its own preferred mixture of fish for frying. Larger fish have to be filleted and cut into bite-sized portions for the tapa table. Spanish housewives try and get the tail piece of a cod or any large fish which has been cut into steaks – they are usually able to get a bargain. The cheeks and throats of cod and hake are particularly prized as little tapa portions. The cheeks can be fried, but the throats should be cooked on their own in a dry pan (skillet) – after a few moments shaking them over the heat, they produce a delicious sticky sauce.

Makes 15–20 tapa mouthfuls   Serves 2 as a starter

250g (8oz) skinned white fish fillets (cod, hake, haddock or monkfish)

2–3 tablespoons milk

3–4 tablespoons seasoned coarse plain (all-purpose) flour (mix in a little fine semolina for a really crisp coating)

oil for shallow-frying (half olive, half sunflower is perfect)

salt

lemon or bitter orange quarters, to serve

Trim the fish fillets into neat bite-sized strips: cut them across diagnolly for extra strength – the cross-grain holds them together.

Dip the fish in the milk and then in the seasoned flour, shaking off any excess.

Heat up the oil for frying. When it is hazed with blue, drop in the fish – not too much at a time so that the temperature of the oil remains high. Fry the fish crisp and golden, turning once. Remove and drain on kitchen paper.

Sprinkle with salt, spear each piece with a cocktail stick and serve with quarters of lemon or bitter orange.

Pickled sardines
Escabeche de sardinas

This recipe is very popular in Roquetas del Mar on the coast of Almería. The pickle originally served to conserve the sardine catch in the days before refrigeration. It remains a popular dish today. The pickled fish will keep for a week in the fridge.

Makes 12–15 tapa portions   Serves 4 as a starter

500 g (1 lb) fresh sardines
  or small herring
2 garlic cloves, sliced
1 bay leaf
150 ml (¼ pint) (⅔ cup)
  white wine vinegar

150 ml (¼ pint) (⅔ cup)
  water
2 tablespoons olive oil
salt and pepper

Preheat the oven to Gas Mark 3/160°C/325°F.

Wash the sardines or herring. Scale with a sharp knife and gut them by slitting the bellies with the knife and pulling out the innards. Trim off the heads and tails. Layer the fish in a shallow casserole, putting the garlic, bay leaf and salt and pepper between the layers. Bring the vinegar and water to the boil and then pour it round the fish. Trickle the oil over the top. Lid or cover with foil.

Bake in the oven for half an hour. Leave to cool. Serve warm or cold, cut into bite-sized pieces and each speared with a cocktail stick.

Grilled (broiled) sardines
Sardinas asadas

This is the most popular way of preparing the fine fat sardines trawled by the inshore fleet. Fresh-caught sardine flash a brilliant rainbow of colour – green, turquoise and scarlet on silver flanks. Don't de-scale the fish for grilling (broiling) – the scales and the natural oil in the skin prevent them sticking.

Makes 8–9 tapa portions   Serves 2–3 as a starter

500 g (1 lb) fresh sardines
1 tablespoon salt

lemon quarters, to serve

Gut the sardines – easily done with your index finger through the soft bellies, or by slitting the bellies with a sharp knife and pulling out the innards. Leave the heads and scales on, and sprinkle the fish with plenty of salt.

Heat up the grill or barbecue until the metal is really hot. Lay on the fish. Grill (or broil) them fiercely, turning once, until the skin blisters black and bubbly. The thicker the fish the longer they will need – 3–4 minutes a side should be ample.

Serve one fish per tapa to eat with the fingers, with a quarter of lemon, and bread for wiping fishy fingers.

Fried anchovies
Boquerones fritos

Spanish cooks have brought the art of frying fish to perfection. The freshness of the fish, the quality of the flour and the salt, and fine clear oil, all contribute to the success of this simple dish. Anchovies and small sardines are the cheapest and most plentiful of Andalucía's inshore harvest, which makes them ideal tapas in seaside bars.

Makes 8–10 tapa mouthfuls   Serves 2 as a starter

250 g (8 oz) fresh anchovies (or small sardines, sprats or large whitebait)	½ teaspoon salt
	oil for frying (a mixture of olive and sunflower is good)
2 tablespoons strong plain (all-purpose) flour	lemon quarters, to serve

Gut the little fish – you can do this just by running your finger down the soft belly, or by slitting the belly with a sharp knife and pulling out the innards. (Sardines will need scaling first.) Behead them or not as you please. Rinse, drain and dry the fish.

Sieve the flour and salt on to a flat plate. Pinch the tails of the fish together in fans of 3 to 5, depending on size. Dust them through the flour, making sure the tails are firmly stuck together.

Heat a finger's depth (1.5 cm/½ inch) of oil in a shallow frying pan (skillet). When the oil is hazed with blue, lay in the fish head-first – only 2 to 3 fans at a time or the temperature drops too fast.

Fry the fish until crisp and golden, turning once. Transfer them on to kitchen paper to drain.

Serve the crisp little fish piping hot, one fan per tapa, accompanied by quarters of lemon.

Monkfish kebabs
Pinchitos de rape

These little kebabs were a speciality of a now-vanished beach bar in Torremolinos, back in those distant days when this popular seaside resort was nothing more than a fishing village. Swordfish can be used instead of the monkfish. You will need some very thin skewers: steel knitting needles are popular in Spain; bamboo skewers are an excellent alternative.

Makes 12–15 tapa mouthfuls   Serves 2 as a starter   (Pictured on page 72)

250 g (8 oz) filleted
  monkfish
1 green pepper
1 tablespoon olive oil
1 tablespoon lemon juice

1 garlic clove, chopped
1 teaspoon cumin seeds
salt and pepper
cubes of bread, to serve

Cut the monkfish into bite-sized cubes. Hull, de-seed and cut the green pepper into matching squares. Thread the monkfish alternating with the green peppers on to skewers.

Combine the oil, lemon juice, garlic, cumin and salt and pepper. Bathe the kebabs in this aromatic marinade and leave for an hour or two.

Remove the kebabs from the marinade and drain them.

Heat a griddle or grill to maximum heat. Grill (broil) the kebabs fiercely until the edges of the pepper blacken.

Serve with a cube of bread speared on the end of each kebab.

Spiced mackerel
Caballa en escabeche

When a fishing fleet finds a shoal of mackerel, it catches them by the boatful. In pre-refrigeration days, spiced pickle-baths were a way not only to conserve the catch for a few extra days, but also to add variety to the diet. Use this pickle to spice leftover cod or haddock in batter, or any leftover fried fish.

Makes 12–14 tapa mouthfuls   Serves 3–4 as a starter

500 g (1 lb) mackerel (or fillets of cod or haddock)
1 heaped tablespoon plain (all-purpose) flour
2 tablespoons olive oil
1 slice of onion
1 garlic clove, sliced
1 small carrot, sliced
1 tablespoon chopped parsley
1 teaspoon oregano
1 bay leaf
4 black peppercorns, crushed
4 tablespoons sherry or wine vinegar
2 tablespoons water
¼ teaspoon cayenne pepper
salt

Gut the mackerel – slit the belly with a sharp knife and pull out the innards – then behead and wipe. Chop it straight across the bone to give 6 or 7 thick slices. Sprinkle the slices with salt and dust them with the flour.

Heat the oil in a shallow frying pan (skillet). When it is blue-hazed, put in the fish – don't let the oil overheat. Fry the cutlets golden (a few minutes only so that the fish remains firm); then transfer them to a wide shallow dish.

If you are using leftover fried fish, start the recipe here.

Fry the onion and garlic gently in the oil which remains in the pan (add a little more if you need it). Stir in the carrot, parsley, oregano, bay leaf and peppercorns. Allow the aromatics to fry gently for a few moments so that the flavours blend. Add the vinegar and water, stir in the cayenne and a little salt, and allow the mixture to bubble up. Scrape in all the bits that stick to the bottom of the pan. Pour this warm scented bath unstrained over the fish.

Cover loosely with a clean cloth, and leave at least overnight in a cool place. This is ready to eat in a day, better in two. Serve a bite-sized piece per tapa, speared with a cocktail stick.

Cuttlefish or squid in its own ink
Chipirones o calamares en su tinta

A Basque speciality, this delicious way of preparing inkfish is popular all over Spain. The cuttlefish is a squid-like creature, but rounder and darker in the body than squid. It has a porous white 'bone' (nature's toothpowder, much appreciated by canaries) instead of the squid's transparent stick. Cuttlefish and squid ink is splendidly black – a kind of oceanic soot which dyes everything it touches. It has a delicate flavour all its own which makes the effort of collecting it worthwhile. The recipe is too time-consuming to be worth making in smaller quantities.

Makes 20–24 tapa mouthfuls   Serves 4 as a starter

500 g (1 lb) small cuttlefish
   or squid
4 tablespoons olive oil
2 onions, chopped
2 garlic cloves, chopped
500 g (1 lb) tomatoes,
   skinned and chopped
   (fresh or canned)

1 tablespoon fresh
   breadcrumbs
1 tablespoon chopped
   parsley
salt and pepper

Wash the cuttlefish or squid thoroughly: they are sandy creatures. Take out the white 'bones', and pull the tentacles and innards away from the body. Look for the silvery ink sacks among the innards. It doesn't matter if you can't find all the sacks – 1 or 2 is quite enough to turn the dish midnight black. Break the sacks into a small sieve placed over a bowl. Reserve the inky liquid.

Remove and discard the beaks, eyes and the soft innards of the fish. Chop the tentacles into small pieces and use them to stuff the hollow bodies.

Warm the oil in a deep-sided frying pan (skillet). Add the onions and garlic and fry gently until they soften. Add the tomatoes. Let the mixture bubble up and cook to a thick sauce.

Lay the stuffed fish in the pan (skillet). Lid and poach the fish gently until soft, adding a little water as necessary so that the juices do not dry out. They will take 20–30 minutes. Transfer the fish to a warm plate while you finish the sauce.

Mash up the ink with the breadcrumbs and parsley. Off the heat stir the ink mixture into the tomato sauce – some people push the sauce through a sieve first. Alternatively, put all the sauce ingredients into a liquidiser and process to a smooth black purée.

Return the sauce to the pan. Lay in the fish. Reheat gently. Taste and add salt and pepper.

Serve warm, one fish and a dab of sauce per tapa, speared with a cocktail stick.

Baked scallops
Vieiras de Santiago de Compostela

The scallop or pilgrim-shell, unlike most of its fellow bi-valves, is a wanderer, propelling itself backwards through the world's oceans in its perpetual search for food. In recognition of this, scallop shells were worn by medieval pilgrims in their hats to indicate that they were on their way to the great shrine of St James of Compostela, in north-western Spain. Because of this, the scallop is a recurrent decorative motif all along Europe's pilgrim routes.

Makes 6 tapa portions   Serves 3 as a starter

6 scallops (in their shells, if possible)
3 tablespoons olive oil
1 garlic clove, chopped
1 onion, chopped finely
1 heaped tablespoon chopped parsley
1 teaspoon plain (all-purpose) flour
1 wine glass of sherry
1 wine glass of water
2 tablespoons grated hard cheese (Manchego or Cheddar)
salt and pepper

Clean the scallops and chop them in half if they are large. Slice them into discs, leaving the corals whole.

Heat 2 tablespoons of the oil. Turn the scallop pieces in the hot oil until the surfaces caramelise a little. Take the fish out and replace with the garlic, onion and parsley. Sprinkle in the flour and add the sherry. Bubble up to evaporate the alcohol, add the water and bubble up again; then return the scallops and reheat. Taste and add salt and pepper. Pile the mixture back into their deep shells or place in individual baking dishes.

Sprinkle with the grated cheese and the remaining trickle of oil. Finish under the grill until gilded and bubbling. Serve one scallop each as a tapa, in its cooking dish.

Grilled (broiled) prawns
Gambas a la parilla

Prawns for grilling (broiling), should be raw when you start. Ready-cooked ones are at their best served cold with mayonnaise (page 31) and/or chopped vegetable sauce (page 38).

Makes 7–8 tapa portions   Serves 2 as a starter   (Pictured on page 90)

250g (8oz) large raw
   prawns (fresh or frozen)
1 tablespoon olive oil

1 tablespoon salt
1 lemon, quartered, to
   serve

Rub the whole prawns, unpeeled and with the heads left on, with a slick of oil. Salt them heavily – plenty of salt on the skin enhances the natural sweetness of the flesh inside.

Heat the grill or barbecue until it until it is sizzling hot. Slap on the prawns. Let them cook, turning once – 2–3 minutes a side should be enough.

Serve them with quarters of lemon, and bread on which to wipe fishy fingers.

Grilled (broiled) oysters
Ostras gratinadas

If you are catering for those who like their oysters raw, do not interfere with their pleasure. Otherwise this is a deliciously simple way of preparing the king of shellfish.

Makes 6 tapa portions   Serves 1–2 as a starter   (Pictured on page 90)

6 oysters
2–3 tablespoons fresh
   breadcrumbs
1 tablespoon chopped
   parsley

1 garlic clove, chopped
   finely
1 tablespoon olive oil
1 lemon, quartered, to
   serve

Carefully open the oysters by levering apart with a knife. Leave them on their deep half-shell.

Sprinkle each oyster with a little hat of breadcrumbs, parsley and garlic. Finish with a trickle of oil. Pop the oysters under the grill until they plump up and sizzle.

Serve one each, speared with a cocktail stick, as a tapa. Accompany with bread and a quartered lemon.

Prawns in garlic and oil (page 94)
Mushroom croquettes (page 139)
Spanish potato omelette (page 66)
Chicken kebabs with fresh tomato sauce (page 127)
Tomatoes stuffed with pine kernels (page 60)

Grilled (broiled) oysters and prawns (page 88)
Asparagus with soft-boiled eggs (page 52)
Peppery potatoes (page 58)
Grilled (broiled) lamb cutlets with garlic mayonnaise (page 104)

Clams in sherry
Almejas en vino de jerez

Shellfish are trucked all over Spain from as far away as the Scottish Hebrides – Spanish cooks like their shellfish alive on the shell and prepare them in simple recipes which make the most of their delicate flavour. This is the classic way to prepare any bi-valve using the native-grown wine of Andalucía.

Makes 12 tapa portions   Serves 2–3 as a starter   (Pictured on page 53)

500 g (1 lb) clams or
  cockles in their shells
1 tablespoon olive oil
1 garlic clove, chopped

1 tablespoon chopped
  parsley
1 wine glass of dry sherry

Wash the shellfish in plenty of cold water, checking over and discarding any which are broken or that don't close when handled. Leave to soak in cold water for an hour or two.

Put the oil to heat in a wide shallow frying pan (skillet) (I use a wok). When the oil is lightly hazed with smoke, toss in the garlic and fry for a moment. Add the parsley and the wine. When it is good and hot, add the shellfish.

Cover with a lid, shaking the pan to redistribute the shells so that all have a chance to cook. If you have no lid, keep moving the clams with a metal drainer. It will take 3–4 minutes for all the shells to open. Discard any that remain closed.

Do not cook them any longer but serve immediately. They should not be reheated or they will be rubbery. They're delicious hot or cold.

Serve 2 or 3 shells as a tapa, sauced with a little of the aromatic juice.

The area where sherry can be made is strictly limited to preserve the quality of real Spanish sherry. It is bordered by Jerez de la Frontera, Puerto de Santa María, and Sanlúcar de Barrameda – a port also well known for being the starting point of Columbus's famous voyage.

Fried squid
Calamares fritos

Squid and cuttlefish, from the hefty *calamar* to the tiny *chipirón*, are perfect material for the frying pan (skillet). This is one of the most popular of tapas. Very small cuttlefish can be cooked whole – they are delicious but must be very fresh, and they spit oily juices all over the cooker. More widely available are the larger squid (they grow up to two feet long), whose milk-white bodies can be cut into neat rings. To prepare whole fish, follow the instructions on page 86.

Makes 12–15 tapa mouthfuls   Serves 2 as a starter   (Pictured on page 126)

250 g (8 oz) prepared squid, cut into rings and short lengths of tentacle
3–4 tablespoons plain (all-purpose) flour
1 egg, beaten
oil for frying (half olive, half sunflower is excellent)
salt
lemon quarters, to serve

Rinse the squid and pat it dry.

Dust each ring through the flour; then dip it into the egg. Do not add salt at this stage: Spanish cooks do not salt squid, cuttlefish or octopus before cooking, believing that salting toughens the flesh. (I will take their word for it – Spanish housewives handle a great deal of squid.)

Heat the frying oil until you can see a faint blue haze rising from the surface. Test the heat with a cube of bread first – it should colour as soon as it is dropped in.

Fry the rings, not too many a time, in the hot oil. Drain and sprinkle with salt. Serve hot, with lemon quarters.

Winkles or whelks with spiced vinegar
Bigarros o bocinas con vinagre

The winkle supplied early man with his tapas – periwinkle shells are found in prehistoric middens all over Europe. In Spain the most widely appreciated sea snail is the Mediterranean spiny *canadilla*, the murex. Winkles and whelks conform to the spirit if not the letter of the delicacy.

Makes 10–12 tapa portions   Serves 3–4 as a starter   (Pictured on page 72)

500 g (1 lb) winkles or
    whelks
1 dried chilli, de-seeded
6 white peppercorns,
    crushed
½ teaspoon crushed
    coriander seeds

1 bay leaf, torn into small
    pieces
¼–½ wine-sized bottle of
    sherry or wine vinegar
salt

If the shellfish is still raw, boil the winkles for 10 minutes in
salted water (the whelks will need 20 minutes at least,
depending on size). Drain and rinse in cold water, and let
them cool.

Meanwhile, put the aromatics into the bottle of vinegar.
The longer this is kept, the better it is.

Serve the shellfish with pins or cocktail sticks and the
spiced vinegar for dipping.

Fisherman's mussels
Mejillones a la marinera

Fresh mussels make the perfect tapa – they are cheap, exactly the
right size for a mouthful, and even come naturally packaged in their
own container. They are very good cold, dressed with a little oil and
a shellful of finely chopped onion, garlic, tomato and pepper.
Cooked, they will keep for several days in the fridge. Make the dish
with clams or any fresh live shellfish instead of the mussels.

Makes 12–16 tapa mouthfuls   Serves 2 as a starter   (Pictured on page 125)

500 g (1 lb) mussels in their
    shells (or cockles or
    clams)
1 tablespoon olive oil
1 garlic clove, chopped
    finely

1 tablespoon chopped
    parsley
1 wine glass of dry sherry
salt

Scrub the mussels and trim off their black beards. Discard
any which do not close when they are handled.

Heat the oil in a wide pan (I use a wok). Throw in the
garlic and let it soften for a moment. Add the parsley and the
sherry and salt. Bubble it up and add the mussels. Lid, turn
up the heat and let the shells open in the steam. Discard any
that don't open.

That's all. Don't reheat them. They're perfect as they are.
Serve one or two shells per tapa.

Octopus in paprika oil
Pulpo a la gallega

This is the speciality of the fishing communities of Galicia on Spain's rocky north-western coast. It can be made with dried octopus – a popular preparation all round the Mediterranean, sold as a leathery tangle of suckered arms. It can be served hot or cold, and keeps for a week in the fridge.

Makes 15–20 tapa mouthfuls   Serves 2 as a starter

500 g (1 lb) small octopus (or cuttlefish or squid)
2 garlic cloves, chopped finely
1 tablespoon paprika
6 tablespoons olive oil
salt and pepper

Wash the fish thoroughly. If you are using squid or cuttlefish, prepare it according to the instructions on page 86. If you are dealing with octopus, bang the creature on a hard board to tenderise it first. Bring a pan of unsalted water to the boil. Dip the octopus in the boiling water three times (this ritual is traditional).

Bring the water back to the boil, put in the octopus or squid, lid and simmer until tender. Small octopus take about 2 hours to cook tender, squid only about 30 minutes.

Meanwhile, make the sauce by blending the rest of the ingredients in a mortar or in a food processor.

Drain the octopus or squid and cut it into bite-sized pieces. Dress the pieces with the oil and paprika sauce, spike with cocktail sticks and accompany with plenty of bread to mop up the aromatic oil.

Prawns in garlic and oil
Gambas al ajillo

This dish is one of the great pleasures of the tapa table. *Anguilas*, baby eels (elvers), are also prepared *al ajillo*. The prawns are served sizzling hot in their individual cooking dish, as a *ración* – a single portion to share. Tapa bars which specialise in these mouth-scalding preparations have little wooden forks so that customers do not burn their tongues. Crab is also excellent prepared in this way – it'll need a splash of sherry or brandy to keep it moist.

Makes 2–3 tapa portions   Serves 1 as a starter   (Pictured on page 89)

2 tablespoons olive oil
1 garlic clove, sliced
1 small dried red sweet
  pepper, de-seeded and
  chopped, or ¼ teaspoon
  cayenne pepper

125 g (4 oz) peeled prawns
salt

Heat the oil in a small shallow casserole over a high heat, or in the oven. When the oil is sizzling, add the garlic and salt. Let it take a little colour and then sprinkle in the pepper and the prawns. Reheat, stirring the prawns quickly in the hot oil.

Serve as soon as the oil is spitting-hot, in the cooking dish, with little wooden forks or wooden cocktail sticks, and bread for mopping up the aromatic oil.

Crayfish with green sauce
Cigalas con salsa verde

This is a speciality of the Casa Antonio Martin on the Malaga seafront beside the bullring. The green sauce is delicious with any cold fish or shellfish. It can be used to dress cold mussels or a seafood salad.

Makes 8 tapa portions   Serves 2 as a starter   (Pictured on page 125)

8 raw crayfish or Dublin
  Bay prawns
salt

THE SAUCE
2 tablespoons olive oil
1 tablespoon sherry or
  wine vinegar or lemon
  juice

4 tablespoons water
1 garlic clove, chopped
  finely
1 tablespoon finely
  chopped spring onion
1 tablespoon finely
  chopped parsley
salt and pepper

Bring a pan of heavily salted water to the boil and throw in the raw crayfish or Dublin Bay prawns. Bring the water back to a rolling boil, and then allow 8 minutes on the boil. Remove the pan from the heat, lid it and leave it for 3 minutes. Drain the crayfish and rinse them with cold water. Leave them to cool in a cold place.

Meanwhile mix the sauce ingredients together and leave to develop the flavours for an hour or so.

Serve the crayfish with the green sauce.

Shrimp fritters
Tortillitas de camarones

These crisp little fritters are sold hot from the frying vat on every street corner of the windswept port of Cádiz. They are made with tiny jumping shrimps, *camarones*, netted in the long sandy shallows which edge the famous salt flats beyond the town. The fritters are very good made with tiny ready-cooked 'grey' shrimps, which need no peeling.

Makes 10–12 small fritters   Serves 2 as a starter

3 tablespoons self-raising
  flour
½ teaspoon salt
6 tablespoons water
2 tablespoons olive oil
¼ teaspoon paprika
1 tablespoon very finely
  chopped onion

1 tablespoon chopped
  parsley
125 g (4 oz) whole tiny
  shrimps or peeled
  shrimps, chopped finely
oil for frying

Sieve the flour and salt into a bowl, and gradually blend in the water and oil until you have a thin batter.

Stir in the paprika, onion and parsley. Fold in the shrimps.

Heat 2 fingers' depth (3 cm/1 inch) of oil in a pan (skillet). When it is lightly smoking, drop in the shrimp batter by the tablespoonful – not too many at a time or the oil temperature will drop. Fry golden and crisp, turning once. Flatten the fritters with a draining spoon as they cook, to make sure the batter is well spread out so that they are crisp all the way through.

Serve piping hot straight from the pan.

Clams in tomato sauce
Almejas en salsa

This recipe is popular in and around the port of Santander in northern Spain. Prawns or sliced squid can be substituted for the shellfish. A knife-point of chilli can be stirred in to spark up the flavour.

Makes 20–24 tapa portions   Serves 2 as a starter

500 g (1 lb) clams in their
  shells (or cockles or
  mussels)
1 tablespoon olive oil
1 tablespoon chopped
  onion
1 garlic clove, chopped

2 tomatoes, skinned and
  chopped
1 teaspoon paprika
1 wine glass of dry sherry
1 tablespoon chopped
  parsley
salt and pepper

Put the shellfish to soak for an hour or two in cold water so
that they spit out any sand. Discard any which are cracked or
that don't close when handled, or whose weight indicates
that they are full of sand.

Warm the oil in a wide shallow pan (a wok is perfect).
Throw in the onion and garlic, and let it fry gently for a few
moments to take colour. Add the tomatoes and paprika.
Turn up the heat, stirring with a wooden spoon as the
tomatoes soften.

Pour in the sherry and bubble up to evaporate the alcohol.
Add the shellfish and turn them in the hot sauce until they
open. Discard any that remain closed. Add the parsley. Taste
and add salt and pepper.

Take them off the heat and serve one each per tapa, with a
topping of the rich sauce.

Griddled razor shells
Navajas a la plancha

These are a neglected delicacy in Britain – razor shells are common
enough round our shores. As a child, I used to find them on the
beach and eat them raw. Griddled only long enough for them to
open, they make a perfect little titbit for a tapa.

Makes 12 tapa mouthfuls   Serves 3 as a starter

12 razor shells   1 lemon, to serve

Soak the molluscs in cold water for an hour or two so that
they spit out any sand.

Heat a griddle or heavy iron frying pan (skillet) until it is
sizzling hot. Griddle the shellfish until they open in their
own steam. Discard any that remain closed.

Remove them immediately from the heat. Serve one each
as a tapa, with a squeeze of lemon.

Basque crab
Changurro

The Basques make this with spider crab, *centolla*, caught off the coast of Guipuzcoa (and all round the coasts of Europe, including the Mediterranean). Spider crabs, as their name suggests, are spiky-bodied, long-legged creatures lacking the characteristic well-developed claws; their meat is deliciously succulent.

Makes 20–24 tapa mouthfuls   Serves 2 as a main course   (Pictured on page 107)

175 g (6 oz) prepared crab meat (in the shell, if possible)
2 tablespoons olive oil
50 g (2 oz) (¼ cup) butter
1 small leek, chopped finely
1 tablespoon chopped onion
1 garlic clove, chopped
1 teaspoon paprika
¼ teaspoon cayenne pepper
1 teaspoon tomato purée
1 small glass of dry sherry
1 tablespoon brandy
1 tablespoon chopped parsley
1 tablespoon fresh breadcrumbs
salt and pepper

Remove the crab meat from its shell (if necessary) and fork the dark and the white meat together.

Warm the oil with half the butter. Add the leek, onion and garlic. Cook the vegetables gently until soft.

Add the crab meat to the pan. When the mixture is bubbling hot, stir in the paprika, cayenne, tomato purée, sherry and brandy and bubble up for 2 or 3 minutes more to evaporate the alcohol. Taste and add salt and pepper.

Return the crab mixture to its shell or place in a small shallow casserole. At this point the crab can be left for later reheating, or even frozen as it is.

Sprinkle with the parsley and breadcrumbs, dot with the remaining butter and pop under a very hot grill for 5 minutes to gild and brown the top. Serve in its dish, with forks.

> *Spain is justly famous for its robust, oak-aged red wines from the Rioja region in the north of Spain. The Domecq family are the largest single vineyard owners in the region.*

Crab with saffron dressing
Centolla a la vinagreta levantina

Crab is delicious cold and simply dressed. This saffron-perfumed vinaigrette is an unusual recipe from Valencia, where seafood and saffron are considered the most natural of partners. Crayfish or large prawns are equally good prepared this way.

Makes 15–20 tapa mouthfuls   Serves 2–3 as a starter

6 crab claws, shelled
4 tablespoons olive oil
1 onion, chopped finely
½ teaspoon cayenne pepper
3–4 saffron threads infused in 1 tablespoon boiling water, or ¼ teaspoon saffron powder

1 small glass of brandy
1 teaspoon sherry or wine vinegar
1 hard-boiled egg, chopped finely
salt

Chop the crab claws into bite-sized pieces.

Heat the oil in a small pan. Add the chopped onion and cook gently for a few minutes until it softens. Stir in the cayenne pepper and saffron and then splash in the brandy. Bubble all up to evaporate the alcohol.

Remove from the heat and add the vinegar. Add the crab pieces and stir in the chopped hard-boiled egg and salt.

Serve warm or cold, in little saucers with forks or cocktail sticks, and bread so none of the fragrant saffron sauce is wasted.

Meat

Pork remains the universal meat of Spain – the omnivorous pig has long been an honoured member of the Spanish rural household. As well as being allowed to range wild through the woods to scavenge for roots and acorns, he eats up the kitchen leftovers, re-cycling anything edible which would otherwise go to waste. The annual pig-killing still provides isolated farming communities with their winter supplies of salt-dried ham and spiced sausage.

In what was once Muslim Spain, which included Andalucía, pork was a dietary taboo until the Christian re-conquest at the end of the fifteenth century. Lamb and mutton, the preferred meat of the Moors, disappeared from the southern menu at that time, although the shepherding uplands continued to enjoy them. As recently as fifteen years ago in my local town of Tarifa, lamb was considered a Moorish taste.

Kid is the great treat among the rural communities of the south. Roasted or as a savoury stew, it marks the high-spot of the country wedding feast, a roofing-out party (a sort of housewarming party), or at any occasion where the food must be special.

Since Andalucía breeds fighting bulls for the ring, beef also figures on the tapa table. During the summer bullfighting season the little villages have a sudden glut of mature beef. Local bars and restaurants make the most of this cheap plenty. Such beef is not the most tender of morsels but the flavour is good, and *carne de lidia* (fighting beef) makes a fine slow-cooked stew. Tough meat from any part of the animal is often sliced into thin steaks – *filetes* – which are garlicked and flash-fried, Chinese-style.

For the rest, offal dishes are often served as tapas in bars and restaurants. Offal is the traditional source of cheap protein for the urban poor, who had no access to those wild harvests available to country people. Variety meats, such as tripe, liver, heart and kidneys, are familiar enough, but the tapa-hunting traveller will certainly come across stranger titbits – thyme-marinated cawl wrapped around vine twigs, and ears and tails and trotters stewed and spiced Moorish-style with cinnamon and cloves.

Meatballs in tomato sauce
Albóndigas en salsa

Moulding meatballs is one of the first culinary tasks Spanish children undertake – small neat fingers are perfect for working the paste and rolling the mixture into little marbles. The proportion of meat to breadcrumbs varies according to the means of the cook. Serve them as a main course, with rice or mashed potato. They can be made well ahead and reheated, and freeze beautifully in their sauce.

Makes 10–12 meatballs   Serves 2 as a main course   (Pictured on page 144)

250 g (8 oz) minced (ground) pork and/or beef

1 egg

2 tablespoons fresh breadcrumbs, soaked in a little water

1 garlic clove, chopped

1 tablespoon chopped parsley

½ teaspoon salt

1 tablespoon plain (all-purpose) flour

1 tablespoon olive oil

pepper

THE SAUCE

1 onion, chopped

500 g (1 lb) tomatoes, skinned and chopped (fresh or canned)

1 wine glass of dry sherry

1 bay leaf

Work the meat, egg, breadcrumbs, garlic and herbs together with the salt and plenty of pepper. Work it some more until the mixture is a firm ball of paste. Divide it into 10–12 marble-sized balls. Roll the balls lightly in the flour.

Heat the oil in a frying pan (skillet). Put in the meatballs and fry them gently for 5–6 minutes, turning them to cook all sides. Remove the meatballs and reserve them.

Now make the sauce. The meat will have released extra fat into the pan, so use that to fry the onion gently until it softens. Add the tomatoes and bubble up fiercely until you have a thick sauce. Add the sherry and bay leaf and heat again to evaporate the alcohol. Return the meatballs to the pan, lid and cook them gently in the sauce for 10–15 minutes.

Serve each meatball with a little sauce, spiked with a cocktail stick.

Grilled (broiled) spiced hamburgers
Hamburguesas a la plancha

This is the universal hamburger, spiced Spanish-style. It is really a flattened meatball, which is perhaps why it achieved instant popularity in Spain. The mixture makes an excellent full-sized hamburger as a main dish, served with crisp french fries fried in olive oil (page 56).

Makes 8 bite-sized hamburgers   *Serves 2 as a main course*   (*Pictured on page 125*)

250 g (8 oz) minced (ground) beef	1 teaspoon ground cumin
1 tablespoon fresh breadcrumbs	1 small egg, beaten lightly
1 garlic clove, chopped	a little olive oil for greasing
1 tablespoon finely chopped onion	salt and pepper
1 tablespoon chopped parsley	bread and quartered lemons, to serve

Work the minced (ground) meat, breadcrumbs, garlic, onion, parsley, cumin, egg and salt and pepper together with your hands, until you have a smooth, slightly sticky mass. Divide the mixture into 8 balls. Flatten them into thin discs.

Heat the griddle or a heavy iron frying pan (skillet). Slick it with the oil. When it is smoking, smack on the hamburgers. Cook them quickly, turning once.

Serve hot on rounds of bread or in tiny buns, and accompany with lemon quarters.

Steaks with blue cheese
Filetes con cabrales

Butchers in Spain are expert at turning a whole beef carcass into fine-cut steaks – *filetes* – the cut most in demand by Spanish housewives. Meat is not jointed, but de-boned and separated into large pieces which follow the muscular structure of the animal. All but the toughest shin is then sliced up into thin steaks, Chinese-style, for flash-frying. This is a popular little tapa in northern Spain.

Makes 4–6 tapa portions   *Serves 2–3 as a starter*   (*Pictured on page 53*)

250 g (8 oz) very thin-cut
lean braising steak
1 tablespoon olive oil
1 garlic clove, chopped
finely

50 g (2 oz) blue cheese,
cubed (Cabrales,
Roquefort or Stilton)
salt and pepper
bread squares, to serve

Trim the steak into bite-sized pieces. Put it to marinate for
10–15 minutes in the olive oil, garlic and salt and pepper.

Heat up a griddle or heavy iron frying pan (skillet). Flash
fry the steaks and put each on a square of bread which will
just accommodate it.

Top each steak with a nugget of the blue cheese. Spike
with a cocktail stick, and serve hot.

Breadcrumbed steaks
Filetes a la milanesa

This is a popular method of making a little meat go further. Pork
steaks can be used instead of beef – I sometimes mix a pinch of herbs
and a little paprika into the coating crumbs for pork. The fillets can
be egg-and-breadcrumbed and then frozen, ready to be fried later.

Makes 10 tapa portions   Serves 2–3 as a main course

250 g (8 oz) very thin-cut
beef steaks
1 heaped tablespoon
seasoned plain (all-
purpose) flour
1 small egg, beaten with 1
tablespoon milk

2 tablespoons fine toasted
breadcrumbs
oil for frying (sunflower
and olive oil mixed is
excellent)
salt and pepper
lemon quarters, to serve

Pat the steaks dry and cut them into bite-sized pieces.
Sprinkle with a little salt and pepper.

Spread the flour on one plate, the egg on a second, the
breadcrumbs on a third. Dust the steaks through the flour,
and then dip them in the egg so that both sides are lightly
slicked. Then coat them in the breadcrumbs, pressing to
make the crumbs stick, and shaking off any excess.

Heat a finger's depth (1.5 cm/½ inch) of oil in a frying pan
(skillet). When it is lightly hazed with smoke, slip in the
breadcrumbed fillets – not all at a time or the oil temperature
will drop. Fry until the breadcrumbs are golden, turning
once. Pork steaks will need a few minutes longer. Continue
until all the steaks are done.

Serve with quartered lemons.

Lamb ribs with paprika
Frite

This simple spicy way with lamb is a speciality of Pedraza near Segovia on Spain's high central plateau. It makes a delicious main course served with rice or mashed potato. Make it ahead if you like – it reheats well and freezes perfectly.

Makes 12–15 tapa portions   Serves 2–3 as a main course

500 g (1 lb) belly of lamb, cut into riblets
2 tablespoons olive oil
3 garlic cloves, crushed with 1 teaspoon salt
1 tablespoon paprika
½ teaspoon marjoram or oregano
1 tablespoon chopped parsley
1 tablespoon wine vinegar
1 wine glass of water

Trim the excess fat from the lamb (not too much, this is a rich, oily little dish), and make sure all the pieces are bite-sized.

Heat the oil in a shallow casserole. Turn the meat pieces in the hot oil. Add the garlic and salt, and fry gently until everything takes a little colour. Stir in the paprika, herbs, vinegar and water.

Bring all to the boil, turn down the heat, lid tightly and leave to simmer very slowly for 1–1¼ hours until the meat is tender and the juices have practically all cooked away. Remove the lid for the final 5 minutes, to evaporate any extra liquid. Drain off any excess fat.

Serve the riblets, one each per tapa, with plenty of bread to mop the fingers.

Grilled (broiled) lamb cutlets with garlic mayonnaise
Chuletas de cordero con ajioli

Spanish home-produced lamb is relatively small, giving cutlets of one single juicy bite. In my favourite tapa bar in Seville where these *chuletas* are a popular luxury tapa, the cook speeds up the grilling (broiling) with a red-hot flat-iron applied to the top side.

Makes 6 tapa portions   Serves 2 as a main course   (Pictured on page 90)

6 small lamb cutlets
weighing about 25–50 g
(1–2 oz) each
1 tablespoon olive oil
1 teaspoon oregano or
marjoram
½ teaspoon pepper

1 teaspoon salt

THE SAUCE
6 tablespoons mayonnaise
(page 31)
2 garlic cloves, crushed

Trim the cutlets neatly. Mix the oil with the oregano or
marjoram, pepper and salt. Rub the cutlets all over with this
mixture. Leave for at least 10 minutes to marinate.

Mix the mayonnaise with the crushed garlic.

Heat up the griddle, grill or barbecue. Grill (or broil) the
cutlets over the fiercest heat possible – they should be
charred on the outside, but still pink and juicy within.

Serve one cutlet per tapa, with a spoonful of the garlic
mayonnaise for dipping.

Pork medallions with lemon and marjoram
Lomo de cerdo con limón y mejorana

The lemon cuts the natural richness of the pork in this simple recipe.
It's a particularly good barbecue meat. Serve it as a main course with
mashed potatoes or a well-flavoured juicy risotto.

*Makes 6 tapa portions   Serves 2–3 as a main course   (Pictured on
page 71)*

6 thin-cut pork medallions
weighing about 25–50 g
(1–2 oz) each
1 tablespoon olive oil
juice of 1 lemon

1 garlic clove, crushed
1 tablespoon marjoram
salt and pepper
rounds of bread, to serve

Rub the pork medallions with the oil, lemon juice, garlic,
herbs, and salt and pepper. Leave them to marinate for 10
minutes.

Heat a griddle, heavy iron frying pan (skillet) or grill. Grill
(broil) the medallions over a very high heat, turning once.
Make sure they are cooked right through.

Serve each medallion on its own round of bread, spiked
with a cocktail stick.

Tripe and chilli with chick-peas
Callos con garbanzos en salsa picante

In Spain, tripe is sold ready-scrubbed, but not yet cooked. This raw material gives the finished dish a much more glutinous, rich juice than if it is made with pre-cooked tripe. However, the chilli-spiked tomato-based sauce in this recipe gives the tripe back some of its flavour. It can be prepared well ahead. If you would like to freeze a portion, leave out the chick-peas – they can go in when you reheat it.

Makes 15–20 tapa mouthfuls   Serves 2 as a main course

250 g (8 oz) ready-cooked tripe
1 small chorizo, or salami with 1 teaspoon paprika (optional)
2 tablespoons olive oil
1 onion, chopped
1 wine glass of dry sherry
500 g (1 lb) tomatoes, skinned and chopped (fresh or canned)
1 bay leaf
1 teaspoon thyme
1 fresh or dried chilli, de-seeded and chopped, or ½ teaspoon cayenne pepper
4 tablespoons cooked chick-peas (fresh or canned)
1 garlic clove, chopped finely
1 tablespoon chopped parsley
salt and pepper

Cut the tripe and the chorizo or salami, if used, into small bite-sized pieces.

Warm the olive oil in a shallow pan. Throw in the chopped onion and fry gently until soft. Add the tripe pieces, chorizo or salami and paprika if used, and the sherry. Bubble up to evaporate the alcohol.

Stir in the tomatoes, bay leaf, thyme and chilli or cayenne. Bring to the boil again, turn down the heat and simmer gently, uncovered, for 20–25 minutes, until the sauce is thick and rich. Stir in the chick-peas, garlic and parsley, and reheat. Cook for another 5 minutes. Taste and add salt and pepper.

Serve with forks and plenty of bread.

Rice salad with pine kernels (page 40)
Deep-fried spatchcocked quails (page 123)
Spiced mincemeat pasties (page 142)
Basque crab (page 98)

Roast pork and crisps (page 112)
Tomatoes with anchovies (page 43)
Beetroot salad (page 42)
Canned sardines with onion (page 29)
Canapés of conserved tuna (page 27)

Venison or beef in red wine
Guiso de venado o buey

This recipe for rich venison stew comes from a little *venta* (small country bar) on the road from Algeciras to Ronda, which skirts the great deer forest of Almoraima, once the largest private estate in Europe. The proprietor made good use of the bounty on his doorstep: the tender fillet was grilled over charcoal in the open fireplace, and the rest went into his famous aromatic *guiso*. The stew makes an excellent main dish, served with rice or baked potatoes. It can be prepared ahead, freezes perfectly, and is even better reheated.

Makes 20–24 tapa mouthfuls   Serves 4–5 as a main course

1 kg (2 lb) stewing venison (or beef)
1 tablespoon plain (all-purpose) flour
4 tablespoons olive oil
1 slice of bacon or salt-cured ham, chopped finely
2 garlic cloves, chopped
1 onion, chopped
1 carrot, chopped
1 celery stick
1 tablespoon paprika (or 1 dried red sweet pepper, de-seeded and torn)
3–4 black peppercorns, crushed
500 ml (18 fl oz) (2¼ cups) red wine
1 large glass of water
a bouquet garni (a sprig of rosemary, 2 bay leaves and a sprig of thyme)
1 teaspoon salt

Trim the meat into bite-sized pieces and dust it with the flour.

Heat the oil in a heavy casserole and fry the meat over a high heat until it takes a little colour. Push the meat to one side and add the bacon or ham, garlic, onion, carrot and celery – cook them gently until they soften and brown. Stir in the paprika and the peppercorns.

Pour in the wine and bubble up. Add enough of the water to just submerge the meat, tuck in the bouquet garni and bring back to the boil. Add the salt.

Lid tightly and leave to simmer very gently on the top of the stove (or in a low oven at Gas Mark 2/150°C/300°F) for 1–1½ hours, until the meat is very tender. Check every now and then and add a little more water if necessary.

Serve with plenty of bread – the juices are delicious.

Marinated griddled pork fillet
Lomo en adobo a la plancha

Spanish housewives can buy sliced, ready-marinated fillets of pork from the butcher for this excellent fast food, which is popular as a tapa all over Spain. Served in a roll, it makes a satisfying lunchtime snack. It's the perfect meat for a barbecue. Make it in larger quantities for freezing after the marinating, ready for cooking as required.

Makes 12–15 tapa portions   Serves 3–4 as a light meal

250 g (8 oz) pork fillet
1 tablespoon paprika
½ teaspoon oregano
½ teaspoon thyme
1 bay leaf
1 garlic clove, crushed with
  1 teaspoon salt

1 tablespoon olive oil, plus
  extra for greasing
rounds of bread and lemon
  quarters, to serve

Dry the pork fillet. Mix the paprika, oregano, thyme, bay leaf, and garlic and salt with the oil. Rub the pork fillet thoroughly with this mixture. Wrap it in foil, and leave it in the fridge overnight at least. The meat can be kept in its marinade for a week – improving daily.

When you are ready to cook, cut the fillet into 8–10 thin medallions – on the diagonal if the fillet is slender.

Heat a griddle or heavy iron pan (skillet) until smoking hot. Oil it lightly. Smack on the pork medallions. Cook them for 5–6 minutes, turning once.

Serve each medallion on a round of bread (a slice of French stick, perhaps) which will just accommodate it. Accompany with quartered lemons.

Lamb's tongues in tomato sauce
Lengua en salsa de tomate

The tongues can be prepared ahead, and reheated in the sauce when you are ready to serve. The dish makes a fine main course – serve it with baked potatoes and a salad. Ox tongue can be treated in the same way.

Makes 15–20 tapa portions   Serves 2–3 as a main course

3–4 lamb's tongues
1 carrot, chopped
½ onion, chopped
1 celery stick, chopped
1 bay leaf
3–4 black peppercorns, crushed
salt

THE SAUCE
2 tablespoons olive oil
2 garlic cloves, chopped

500 g (1 lb) tomatoes, skinned and chopped (fresh or canned)
1 wine glass of dry sherry
½ teaspoon thyme
salt and pepper

TO SERVE
1 tablespoon toasted slivered almonds or pine kernels
small rounds of fried bread

Rinse the lamb's tongues. Put them in a saucepan with enough water to cover them. Bring to the boil, skim and add the carrot, onion, celery, bay leaf and peppercorns and salt. Lid and leave to simmer for about 1–1½ hours, until the tongues are tender. Remove them and drain. When they are cool enough, peel the tongues – the thick skin comes off quite easily – and remove any little bones. Cut the tongues into slices.

Meanwhile make the sauce. Warm the oil in a shallow pan, and throw in the garlic. Let it soften and take colour. Add the tomatoes and fry them until they melt. Add the sherry and bubble up. Stir in the thyme. Cook over a gentle heat until you have a thick sauce. Taste and add salt and pepper.

Lay the tongue slices in the sauce and bring all gently back to the boil.

Serve each slice on a piece of fried bread, with a little of the sauce spooned over, and a few slivered almonds or pine kernels on top.

111

Roast pork and crisps
Pata de cerdo al horno con patatas fritas

Big-city tapa bars with a high turnover often take pride in displaying a fine cold roast leg of pork. In my local bar by the port in Algeciras, it was the Saturday special, served on freshly-made potato crisps supplied from a frying kiosk on the pavement outside. It's a delicious way of serving leftovers from the Sunday joint.

Makes 6 tapa portions   Serves 2–3 as a starter   (Pictured on page 108)

6 very thin slices of roast pork
6 tablespoons crisps, preferably home-made (page 26)
1 garlic clove, sliced
1 tablespoon olive oil
1 teaspoon salt

Lay each slice of roast pork on a bed of crisps.
Fry the garlic in the olive oil and scatter it on the meat. Finish with a good sprinkle of salt.

Veal kidneys with sherry
Riñones al jerez

Kidneys cooked in sherry, along with the tortilla (page 66), is the dish most frequently found in Andalucía's tapa bars. Cheap and delicious, it is easy to prepare, can be reheated quickly and freezes well. Serve it as a main course, with rice or mashed potatoes – I love it with french fries fried in olive oil (page 56).

Makes 15–20 tapa mouthfuls   Serves 2 as a main course

1 calves' kidney, trimmed of fat and veins
1 teaspoon sherry or wine vinegar for soaking
2 tablespoons lard (shortening) or olive oil
1 onion, chopped
1 garlic clove, crushed
1 teaspoon paprika
1 tablespoon fresh breadcrumbs
1 tablespoon chopped parsley
1 wine glass of dry sherry
1 wine glass of water
salt and pepper

Slice the kidney into bite-sized pieces and put it to soak in water mixed with the vinegar for 20–30 minutes, to rid it of any ammoniac taste. Or, if you are in a hurry, scald the kidney slices with boiling water.

Warm the lard (shortening) or oil in a shallow casserole. Put in the chopped onion and crushed garlic and let them soften for a moment. Add the kidneys and turn them in the hot oil. Stir in the paprika; then the breadcrumbs and parsley. Pour in the sherry and bubble up to evaporate the alcohol. Add the water, stir well and bring back to the boil.

Lid tightly, turn down the heat, and simmer gently for 25–30 minutes, until the kidneys are tender and the sauce well-thickened. Taste and add salt and pepper.

Serve as a tapa in small portions, with a fork each and plenty of bread to mop up the delicious juices.

Note: this dish also works wonderfully well made with chicken livers.

Griddled marinated lamb's kidneys
Riñones a la plancha

Lambs' kidneys make a perfect bite-sized tapa. Marination in lemon and herbs gives a delicious Mediterranean flavour. The kidneys can be done on a barbecue or under the grill.

Makes 12 tapa portions   Serves 4 as a starter

6 lamb's kidneys, skinned
  and halved lengthways
juice of 1 lemon
1 garlic clove, chopped
2 tablespoons olive oil
1 teaspoon oregano or
  marjoram

1 tablespoon chopped
  parsley
salt and pepper
bread rounds and lemon
  quarters, to serve

Remove the fatty little core in each kidney half. Put the kidneys to marinate for at least 10 minutes in the lemon juice, garlic, oil, herbs and salt and pepper.

Preheat a griddle or heavy iron pan (skillet). Griddle the kidneys over a fierce heat, turning once. They should be charred outside, but still pink and juicy inside.

Serve on small rounds of bread (delicious if you toast it on the griddle), accompanied by quarters of lemon.

> *Wine has probably been produced in the Jerez region for around three thousand years, when the Phoenicians or the Greeks first brought vines to the area and found that they flourished.*

Moorish kebabs
Pinchitos morunos

These little kebabs are a great *feria* treat in Andalucía. In Algeciras, my home town for ten years, *feria* was at the end of June, and it always rained for at least two of the carnival's five days. Each year the same fez-hatted *pinchito* (kebab) man took up temporary residence at one end of a beer and wine wholesaler's pavement bar. We would order cold half bottles of dry sherry from the wine merchant, and negotiate separately for the delicious Moroccan-spiced *pinchitos*, grilled over a charcoal-fuelled barbecue. The *pinchitos* came on long steel knitting-needles which we were honour-bound to return.

Makes 8 kebabs   Serves 4 as a starter   (Pictured on page 53)

250 g (8 oz) diced pork or lamb (lamb's heart and pig's kidneys sometimes replace)
2 tablespoons olive oil
1 teaspoon paprika
½ teaspoon ground turmeric
½ teaspoon ground cumin
½ teaspoon thyme
1 tablespoon chopped parsley
½ teaspoon salt
½ teaspoon pepper
8 cubes of bread, to serve

Check over the meat – all the pieces should be neatly trimmed and no bigger than ordinary dice. Mix together the oil, spices, herbs and seasoning, and turn the meat cubes in this marinade. Leave in a cool place overnight.

Thread the meat on to 8 skewers – 6–7 little pieces each. Heat up the grill or barbecue. Grill (or broil) the kebabs over a very high heat, turning them frequently, until well-browned but still juicy.

Serve hot on their skewers, with a cube of bread speared on the end of each.

Spiced casserole of lamb or kid
Caldereta de cordero o chivo

This method of thickening a stew with breadcrumbs and liver was common in medieval cookery. The recipe is from Malaga, where Moorish culinary influences remain strong.

Makes 12–15 tapa portions   Serves 3–4 as a main course

500 g (1 lb) stewing lamb or kid, removed from the bone
1 wine glass of sherry
a sprig of thyme
1 bay leaf
6 tablespoons olive oil
125 g (4 oz) lamb's liver (in 1 piece)
2 garlic cloves, crushed with ½ teaspoon salt
2 tablespoons fresh breadcrumbs
juice and grated rind of 1 lemon
salt and pepper

Trim the lamb or kid into bite-sized cubes. Put the cubed meat into a saucepan with the sherry, herbs and salt and pepper, and enough water to submerge it. Bring to the boil, skim, add the oil, turn down the heat, and simmer for 20 minutes.

Add the liver (still in 1 piece), bring back to the boil, turn down to simmer and cook for 15 minutes.

Take out the liver. Test the cubed meat – if it is not yet tender, leave it to simmer until it is.

Meanwhile chop the liver roughly and put it in a blender with the garlic and salt, breadcrumbs, ¼ teaspoon pepper and a ladleful of the cooking liquor from the meat. Process to a thick sauce.

Stir the sauce into the meat. Reheat and simmer gently for another 10 minutes. Take off the heat and stir in the lemon juice.

Serve in individual earthenware casseroles, with a sprinkle of the grated lemon rind each. Accompany with plenty of bread to mop up the delicious juices.

> Half bottles of La Ina are available, which are the perfect size for two or three people to enjoy with tapas.

Casserole of lamb or kid with saffron
Caldereta de chivo o cordero

This is a succulent way with a shoulder of lamb. If you use kid, the juices will be stickier and richer. The dish can be prepared in advance and freezes beautifully. It is only worth making in reasonable quantities, and makes a good main course – I love it with sauté potatoes and a salad.

Makes 20–24 tapa portions   Serves 4 as a main course

1 small shoulder of lamb or
   ¼ whole kid, chopped
   into portions through
   the bone
3 tablespoons olive oil
1 large onion, sliced
4 garlic cloves, chopped
1 wine glass of white wine
   or dry sherry
1 wine glass of water
1 bay leaf
3 saffron threads, infused
   and crushed in 1
   tablespoon boiling water
1 lemon, sliced thinly
1 teaspoon ground
   cinnamon
salt and pepper
fried bread, to serve

Trim the lamb or kid into bite-sized pieces, bones and all.
Heat the oil in a casserole which will comfortably
accommodate the meat. Turn the pieces in the hot oil until
they take a little colour. Push the meat to one side and fry
the onion and garlic in the oil. Pour in the wine and bubble
all up. Add the water, bay leaf, saffron with its water, lemon
slices, cinnamon and salt and pepper.

Bring all back to the boil. Turn down the heat and lid
tightly. Simmer gently on top of the stove (or in the oven at
Gas Mark 2/150°C/300°F) for 1–1¼ hours, until the meat is
tender and falling off the bone.

Serve with squares of fried bread and small forks.

Spiced oxtail stew
Estofado de rabo de buey

This rich Moorish-spiced stew is a speciality of Cordoba. Oxtail
always features on the menu in leather-working areas, an industry
for which Cordoba has long been world-famous. The skins for the
trade come in with the tail of the animal still attached, affording a
tasty free morsel for the leather-worker's pot. The stew is better
when reheated, and freezes perfectly.

*Makes 15–20 tapa portions   Serves 3–4 as a main course   (Pictured on
page 144)*

1 whole oxtail, cut into its
   sections
2 tablespoons olive oil
1–2 slices of streaky bacon,
   chopped
1 large onion, chopped
2 garlic cloves, crushed
   with 1 teaspoon salt
1 celery stick, chopped
1 carrot, chopped
1 tablespoon paprika
1 teaspoon ground
   cinnamon
½ teaspoon pepper
3–4 cloves
1 bay leaf
2 wine glasses of red wine
2 wine glasses of water

Wipe and trim the excess fat off the oxtail. Heat the oil in a casserole which will comfortably accommodate all the pieces.

Turn the oxtail pieces in the hot oil. Remove them. Put in the bacon, onion, garlic and salt, celery and carrot and fry gently until the vegetables soften.

Return the oxtail to the casserole, and add the aromatics and the red wine. Allow all to bubble up. Add the water and bring back to the boil. Lid tightly and leave to cook on a very low heat (or in the oven at Gas Mark 2/150°C/300°F) for 3–4 hours, until the meat is practically falling off the bones. Check from time to time, and add more water if necessary. Serve the stew in its dish, with small forks and bread.

Grilled (broiled) pig's trotters with garlic and parsley
Patas de cerdo con ajo y perejil

Pig's trotters are much appreciated all over Europe. They make a cheap and delicious meal, needing only long slow cooking to soften them – otherwise preparation time is minimal. The trotters can be prepared ahead and grilled (broiled) when you are ready. The dish makes a delicious, cheap main course.

Makes 16 tapa portions   Serves 3–4 as a main course

4 pig's trotters, split lengthways	2–3 tablespoons fresh breadcrumbs
1 onion	1 tablespoon chopped parsley
1 carrot	
1 bay leaf	1 garlic clove, chopped
4 black peppercorns, crushed	2 tablespoons olive oil
1 wine glass of sherry	salt and pepper

Wash the pig's trotters and scrub them well. Tie them back together in pairs. Put them in a saucepan which will just accommodate them, along with the onion, carrot, bay leaf and crushed peppercorns. Pour in the sherry and enough water to submerge the trotters to a depth of 1 finger (1.5 cm/ ½ inch). Add a teaspoon of salt.

Bring to the boil, and boil the trotters steadily for half an hour. Top up with boiling water, turn down the heat, lid tightly and leave to simmer very gently for 5 hours, until the trotters are soft and the bones are dropping out. Check the water level every now and then, and add boiling water.

Let the trotters cool in their liquid in the cooking pan. Remove and drain them. Arrange them in a grill pan. Sprinkle with the breadcrumbs, parsley, garlic and salt and pepper, and trickle over the oil.

Reheat in the oven, and then finish them under the grill to gild and crisp the topping.

Liver pâté
Pastel de hígado

This is a useful standby which can be eaten hot or cold. It freezes well and can be prepared well ahead. Serve it as a main dish, hot with mashed potatoes in the winter, cold with a salad in the summer.

Makes 8–10 tapa portions   Serves 4–6 as a starter

500 g (1 lb) pig's liver
175 g (6 oz) lean pork
75 g (3 oz) streaky bacon
1 wine glass of white wine
1 tablespoon chopped
  parsley
1 tablespoon chopped
  onion
1 garlic clove, chopped
1 tablespoon lard
  (shortening)
1 egg, beaten lightly
grated rind of 1 lemon
2 tablespoons fresh
  breadcrumbs
1 bay leaf
pepper

Preheat the oven to Gas Mark 4/180°C/350°F.

Mince the liver, pork and bacon together; then mix in the wine and parsley and plenty of pepper. Fry the onion and the garlic gently together in half the lard (shortening) until they soften. Mix the contents of the frying pan (skillet) with the minced (ground) meat mixture, beaten egg, lemon rind and breadcrumbs: use your hands – they are the most useful kitchen implements.

Thoroughly grease a deep earthenware dish with the rest of the lard (shortening). Put in the meat mixture, lay the bay leaf on the top, and cover with foil.

Cook in the oven for 1–1¼ hours, until the juices run clear when a skewer is pushed into the middle.

To serve it hot, cut it in bite-sized squares and accompany with home-made tomato sauce (page 101). To serve it cold, leave it under a weight overnight; then serve it with pickled gherkins and stuffed olives.

Chicken and game

Throughout Spain chicken is an important source of protein. The housewives of peasant-farming communities keep hens primarily for eggs, but the young cockerels are fattened up for the pot. Small and well-flavoured, chicken remains a Sunday treat in rural communities, and a delectable addition to the tapa table on special occasions. Often combined with well-flavoured pot-herbs and vegetables, both to bulk up the meat and add flavour, one chicken can be made to feed a surprising number of people. Everything goes into the pot – including the neck and giblets – while the head and feet are carefully scrubbed and consigned to the simmering soup-cauldron.

Game is plentiful in Spain's forests and plains – rabbits, small birds, snails and, particularly in the Levante, frogs, are a bounty still to be collected from the wild.

All these relatively lean meats benefit from the marination in herbs, wine and olive oil which is a characteristic of the best of Spanish culinary tradition.

Spiced grilled (broiled) chicken
Pollo en adobo a la plancha

This delicious marinated chicken was my children's favourite birthday barbecue when we all lived in Spain. They could do the preparation themselves – from spicing the chicken to building the fire over which we balanced a makeshift barbecue, made with a grid from the oven resting on a few bricks.

Makes 15 tapa portions   Serves 3–4 as a main course

500 g (1 lb) chicken joints
2 tablespoons olive oil
1–2 garlic cloves, crushed
1 tablespoon paprika
1 tablespoon marjoram
1 teaspoon ground cumin
1 teaspoon crushed
   coriander seeds
1 teaspoon salt
½ teaspoon pepper
½ lemon, sliced

Chop the chicken into 10 bite-sized pieces, following the instructions below. Mix the oil with the garlic, spices, herbs and seasoning, and rub the chicken pieces with the mixture. Add the lemon slices and leave all to marinate, overnight in the fridge if possible.

   Brush off the loose bits of marinade. Grill (broil) the chicken pieces over or under the fiercest possible heat. They should be deliciously charred outside, but still juicy inside.

Chicken with red sweet peppers
Pollo al chilindrón

A succulent dish from Zaragoza in Aragon, this scarlet-sauced chicken is popular all over Spain. Serve it with rice or mashed potatoes as a main course. The Aragonese also prepare their fine tender lamb in the same way. It reheats perfectly, and freezes well.

Makes 10 tapa portions   Serves 3–4 as a main course   (Pictured on page 126)

500 g (1 lb) chicken joints
   (about ½ chicken)
4 tablespoons olive oil
1 garlic clove, crushed
1 onion, chopped
75 g (3 oz) salt-dried ham
   or lean bacon, diced
2 red sweet peppers (or 4
   dried), hulled, de-seeded
   and sliced lengthways
500 g (1 lb) tomatoes,
   skinned and chopped
   well
salt and pepper

Cut the chicken joints into small pieces directly across the bone – drumsticks into 2, thighs into 2, wings into 2, breast into 4. I do this with a heavy knife tapped through the bone by a sharp blow with a hammer.

Heat the oil in a deep casserole. Put in the chicken pieces, garlic and onion and cook them gently until they take a little colour. Push to one side and add the ham or bacon and the peppers. Fry them for a few moments. Put in the tomatoes and bubble it all up.

Turn down the heat, lid tightly and simmer for 25–30 minutes until the chicken is tender and the sauce well-reduced – remove the lid at the end of the cooking time and allow the mixture to bubble up and concentrate the juices. Taste and add salt and pepper.

Serve with forks and plenty of bread for the juices.

Chicken with garlic
Pollo al ajillo

The classic Andaluz country housewife's way with a young barnyard cockerel or a rabbit from the rosemary-scented cistus scrub, this recipe depends on perfect raw ingredients. It's my family's favourite chicken dish, and makes an excellent main course.

Makes 15 tapa portions   Serves 3–4 as a main course

500 g (1 lb) chicken or
  rabbit joints
1 tablespoon seasoned
  plain (all-purpose) flour
8 tablespoons olive oil (it
  must be olive oil)

6 garlic cloves, chopped
  roughly
1 wine glass of dry sherry
salt and pepper

Chop up the joints into smaller, bite-sized pieces, following the instructions above. Dust these pieces with the seasoned flour.

Heat the olive oil in a heavy frying pan (skillet). Put in the chicken and garlic and turn the pieces in the hot oil until they are well browned. Pour in the sherry and bubble it up. Taste and add salt and pepper.

Turn down the heat, lid loosely and leave to simmer gently on a low heat for 20–30 minutes, until the chicken is cooked through but still moist and tender, and the juices have practically evaporated, leaving a delicious garlicky oil as the sauce.

Serve with forks and plenty of bread.

121

Turkey with lemon and saffron
Pavo en pepitoria

The turkey was imported to Spain from the New World, along with such staples as the potato, haricot and butter beans, sweet and chilli peppers, and the tomato. It's hard to imagine what Europe ate before Columbus made landfall.

Makes 15–20 tapa mouthfuls   Serves 3–4 as a main course

250 g (8 oz) boneless turkey breast
2 tablespoons pork lard (shortening)
½ slice of bread
1 garlic clove, chopped
a sprig of parsley
1 bay leaf
½ teaspoon ground cinnamon
¼ teaspoon ground cloves
1 teaspoon paprika
3–4 saffron threads, soaked in 1 tablespoon boiling water
1 tablespoon lemon juice
3 tablespoons water
1 tablespoon chopped onion

Cut the turkey meat into bite-sized portions.

Heat the lard (shortening) in a frying pan (skillet). Fry the bread and the garlic until both are golden. At the end, toss in the parsley and bay leaf and fry them for a moment. Transfer to a food processor or a mortar. Process or pound to a thick sauce with the spices, saffron, lemon juice and water.

Gently fry the turkey pieces and the onion in the lard (shortening) which remains in the pan. When the turkey is a little browned and the onions are soft, stir in the thick sauce. Bubble up and then lid and turn down the heat. Simmer gently until the turkey is cooked – 10–15 minutes. Add a little more water if the sauce dries out.

Serve hot in individual casseroles, with forks.

Breadcrumbed chicken
Pollo rebozado

Spicy morsels of breadcrumbed chicken make delightful party tapas. For a main dish, use a whole jointed chicken, back and all, chopped into bite-sized pieces with the bones left in – it'll yield six full portions.

Makes 8 tapa mouthfuls   Serves 2 as a main course   (Pictured on page 143)

250 g (8 oz) boneless chicken	3 tablespoons fine toasted breadcrumbs
2 tablespoons seasoned plain (all-purpose) flour	1 teaspoon paprika
	1 teaspoon thyme
1 egg, beaten with 1 tablespoon milk	oil for frying
	pepper

Cut the chicken into 8 walnut-sized nuggets. Put the pieces and the seasoned flour in a bag and shake them up to lightly coat the chicken with the flour. Shake off any excess.

Dip the nuggets in the egg-and-milk. Season the breadcrumbs with the paprika, thyme and a little pepper, and roll the nuggets in this mixture.

Heat 2 fingers depth (3 cm/1 inch) of oil until lightly hazed with smoke. Put in the chicken pieces (not too many at a time) and fry, turning them once, until the coating is crisp and the chicken cooked through. The oil should not be too hot as the chicken must be thoroughly cooked by the time the breadcrumbs are golden.

Drain on kitchen paper, and serve with cocktail sticks.

Deep-fried spatchcocked quails
Codornices con ajo

Farmed quail have now replaced little wild birds on the Spanish menu. This is how they are prepared in the seaside *chozo* (small bar) at Punta Paloma near Tarifa, the southernmost point of Europe, and for many years my local market town.

Makes 4 large tapa portions   Serves 2 as a main course   (Pictured on page 107)

4 quail	oil for frying (olive with
1 tablespoon sherry	sunflower is good)
4 garlic cloves, chopped roughly	salt and pepper

Split the quails right down the back, from vent to neck. Flatten them like squashed frogs. Put them to marinate in the sherry, garlic, and salt and pepper for a few hours. Drain and pat them dry.

Heat enough oil to submerge the birds completely. When it is lightly hazed with blue, put in the quail. It will spit, so be careful. Fry the birds until the skin and all the little bones are brown and crisp.

Sprinkle with salt and serve on thick slices of bread.

Quail with parsley and garlic
Codornices a la bilbaína

Farmed quail provide a succulent replacement for the *chimbos* – all manner of little songbirds – which were prepared to this recipe from Bilbao.

Makes 4 tapa portions   Serves 2 as a main course

50 g (2 oz) (¼ cup) butter	1 garlic clove, chopped
2 tablespoons olive oil	2 tablespoons chopped
4 quail, cleaned and halved	parsley
2 tablespoons fresh	
breadcrumbs	

Heat the butter and oil in a heavy frying pan (skillet). Put in the halved birds and fry them gently, turning once, until they are golden brown all over and cooked right through – about 10 minutes in all.

Take out the birds. Fry the breadcrumbs, garlic and parsley in the butter and oil which remains.

Sprinkle the birds with this crisp fragrant topping, and serve them hot, to be eaten with the fingers.

Spiced pigeons
Pichones a la toledana

A recipe from Toledo on the central plateau, the sharp sauce contrasts deliciously well with the pigeons' gamey flavour. For a main course, serve one per person, with a side helping of potatoes fried in olive oil (page 56).

Makes 16 tapa portions   Serves 4 as a main course

8 tablespoons olive oil	2 wine glasses of dry sherry
4 pigeons, cleaned and	1 tablespoon sherry or
quartered	wine vinegar
2 onions, chopped	2 bay leaves
16 garlic cloves	salt and pepper
(unskinned)	

Heat the oil in a heavy casserole. Put in the pigeon quarters and turn them in the hot oil. Add the onions and whole garlic cloves and fry them for a moment. Pour in the sherry

Crayfish with green sauce (page 95)
Cod's roe salad (page 34)
Fisherman's mussels (page 93)
Chard leaves dressed with vinegar (page 59)
Grilled (broiled) spiced hamburgers (page 102)

Fried squid (page 92)
Eggs with mayonnaise (page 33)
Aubergine (eggplant) fritters (page 50)
Chicken with red sweet peppers (page 120)
Chicory and blue cheese (page 43)

and the vinegar and tuck in the bay leaves. Add salt and pepper.

Bring all to the boil, turn down the heat, lid tightly and leave to simmer for 40–50 minutes, until the pigeons are quite tender.

Take off the lid towards the end and evaporate all the juices, leaving the pigeons bathed in aromatic oil.

Serve each quarter with bread. Make sure each person has a garlic clove – creamy and gentle-flavoured when slow-cooked like this. Pop it straight into your mouth from its papery covering.

Chicken kebabs with fresh tomato sauce
Pinchos de pollo con salsa picada

Chicken breasts marinated in oil, garlic, marjoram and lemon have a deliciously sharp flavour. This is a good meat for the barbecue. Serve it with rice and a salad as a main dish in the summer.

Makes 8 tapa portions   Serves 2 as a main course   (Pictured on page 89)

2 boneless chicken breasts
2 tablespoons olive oil
1 garlic clove, crushed
1 tablespoon lemon juice
1 tablespoon chopped
  marjoram or oregano
8 cubes of bread
salt and pepper

THE SAUCE
1 tablespoon finely
  chopped onion

2 tablespoons finely
  chopped cucumber
3 tablespoons finely
  chopped tomato
1 tablespoon sherry or
  wine vinegar
1 tablespoon fresh
  breadcrumbs
1 small glass of water

Divide the chicken breasts lengthways into 4, giving 8 pieces in all. Skewer the strips lengthways. Put them to marinate for a few hours in the oil, garlic, lemon and marjoram or oregano, with a seasoning of salt and pepper.

Mix all the sauce ingredients together and leave them in a cool place to marry the flavours and swell the breadcrumbs.

Grill (or broil) the kebabs on a barbecue, griddle or under the grill. Serve on the skewers, with a cube of bread speared on the end, and a spoonful of the sauce.

Sweet and sour rabbit
Cochefrito de conejo

A speciality of Cordoba, the vinegar balances the natural sweetness of the meat. The dish is also very good made with lamb or kid. Serve it with baked potatoes as a winter main course, or with rice and a salad in the summer.

Makes 10–12 tapa portions   Serves 3–4 as a main course

500 g (1 lb) rabbit joints	1 teaspoon paprika
6 tablespoons olive oil	1 wine glass of water
2 garlic cloves, crushed	1 tablespoon sherry or
½ teaspoon pepper	wine vinegar
½ teaspoon salt	

Trim the rabbit into smaller joints, until you have 10–12 pieces. Heat the oil in a casserole and put in the rabbit and the garlic. Fry until all takes a little colour. Add the seasonings, paprika, water and vinegar.

Bring all to the boil, turn down the heat, cover, and leave to simmer for 30–40 minutes, until the liquid has all boiled away and the rabbit is left gently frying in its oil.

Serve spiked with cocktail sticks.

Rabbit with chocolate
Conejo a la ampurdanesa

One of the most famous and delightful dishes of the Spanish kitchen, this is a direct result of the Spanish involvement in Mexico, where chocolate was used, as here, as a spice. It was also, sweetened and flavoured with vanilla, the favourite drink of the Aztecs, long before Europe ever discovered the pleasure. Cook this dish ahead and reheat it if you like. It freezes well.

Makes 12–16 tapa portions   Serves 3–4 as a main course

500 g (1 lb) rabbit joints	1 wine glass of water
1 tablespoon seasoned	125 g (4 oz) (1 cup) ground
plain (all-purpose) flour	hazelnuts or almonds
100 g (3½ oz) streaky	1 square of plain dark
bacon, diced	chocolate
12 pickling onions	salt and pepper
1 wine glass of red wine	

Joint the rabbit into 12–16 small pieces and roll them in the seasoned flour. In a heavy casserole, melt the bacon until the fat runs. Add the rabbit pieces and the onions and turn them in the hot fat to take colour.

Pour in the wine and water and allow it to bubble up. Turn down the heat, lid tightly and simmer gently for 20–30 minutes, until the rabbit is nearly tender. Stir in the nuts and the chocolate and cook for another 10 minutes, until the sauce is rich and thick. Taste and add salt and pepper.

Serve the rabbit pieces in individual shallow casseroles, with bread to mop up the delicious dark juices.

Potted game
Morteruelo

This is much like English potted meats, of which it may well be the ancestor. Royal marriages in medieval times brought Spanish princesses and their cooks and culinary habits to the courts of England.

Makes 8–10 tapa portions   Serves 4–6 as a starter

500 g (1 lb) mixed cooked
  game (partridge, hare
  and rabbit)
250 g (8 oz) sliced pig's,
  lamb's or calves' liver
50 g (2 oz) streaky bacon,
  chopped finely
1 wine glass of dry sherry

½ teaspoon paprika
¼ teaspoon ground cloves
½ teaspoon ground
  cinnamon
2 tablespoons pine kernels
  or almonds
salt and pepper

Pick over the game, removing any bones and skin. Put the liver slices and bacon in a small pan, with the sherry and enough water to just cover the liver. Bring to the boil. Add the spices and salt and pepper, lid tightly and simmer for 15–20 minutes, until the liver is cooked through.

Put the game meat, liver and bacon into a blender with the pine kernels or almonds, and process with enough of the cooking liquid to give a thick soft paste. Taste and add salt and pepper. Pot and leave to cool.

Serve with hot bread.

Snails in tomato sauce
Caracoles en salsa

Snails are a very popular tapa in small village bars, as the ingredients can be gathered free from the countryside. Two kinds are collected – large ones familar from the French snail dishes, and tiny winkle-sized snails which pass the summer on thorny thistles for protection in the heat.

Makes 20–24 tapa portions   Serves 4 as a starter

4 tablespoons olive oil
1 onion sliced finely
1 tablespoon paprika
500 g (1 lb) tomatoes, skinned and chopped (fresh or canned)
a bouquet garni (1 bay leaf, a sprig of rosemary and a sprig of thyme)
500 g (1 lb) ready-cooked snails (in or out of their shells)
1 tablespoon toasted breadcrumbs
1 tablespoon chopped parsley
salt and pepper

Heat 3 tablespoons of the oil in a shallow pan and gently fry the onion for a few moments. Add the paprika, tomatoes and bouquet garni. Bubble up to soften the tomatoes and thicken the sauce. Add the snails. Simmer all together for 20 minutes, until the sauce and the snails are well married. Taste and add salt and pepper.

Transfer to individual casseroles. Top each with a sprinkle of the breadcrumbs and parsley and a trickle of the remaining oil. Flash under the grill to gild the topping. Serve hot, with cocktail sticks to hook the snails, and plenty of bread to mop up the juices.

Snails with ham and chorizo
Caracoles a la burgalesa

A tasty northern way with snails, this is a speciality of Burgos – a town which also has a reputation for good cheese and delicious junket.

Makes 20–24 tapa portions   Serves 4 as a starter

4 tablespoons olive oil
2 garlic cloves, chopped
50 g (2 oz) salt-dried ham
   or lean bacon, chopped
75 g (3 oz) chorizo, or
   salami with 1 teaspoon
   paprika, cubed small
1 tablespoon fresh
   breadcrumbs
1 small chilli, de-seeded
   and chopped
1 wine glass of white wine
500 g (1 lb) snails in their
   shells
1 tablespoon chopped
   parsley
salt and pepper

Heat the oil in a frying pan (skillet). Add the garlic and let it fry for a few moments to soften. Stir in the ham or bacon and chorizo or salami and fry that a little. Add the paprika if using salami. Stir in the breadcrumbs and the chilli and the wine. Allow all to bubble up and then add the snails. Turn them in the hot sauce. Add salt and pepper to taste.

Lid and cook gently for 20 minutes to develop all the flavours. Finish with the chopped parsley.

Serve with forks and plenty of bread.

Frogs' legs
Ancas de rana

Spain shares a taste for frogs' legs with its northern neighbours. This simple recipe is from Albuferia, where the marshes have plentiful supplies of the raw materials.

Makes 8 tapa portions   Serves 2 as a starter

4 pairs of frogs' legs,
   separated
2 tablespoons dry sherry
1 teaspoon lemon juice
a sprig of thyme
1 garlic clove, chopped
4 tablespoons olive oil
1 egg, beaten lightly
2 tablespoons fresh
   breadcrumbs
1 tablespoon chopped
   parsley
salt and pepper
lemon quarters, to serve

Put the frogs' legs to marinate for an hour in the sherry, lemon juice, thyme, garlic, salt and pepper and 1 tablespoon of the olive oil.

Drain the frogs' legs and dip them in the egg. Mix the breadcrumbs with the parsley. Dip the frogs' legs in the breadcrumbs.

Heat the rest of the oil in a frying pan (skillet). Fry the frogs' legs until the coating is crisp and golden. Serve with lemon quarters.

Croquettes, pasties and pies

These little snacks are a way of stretching small quantities of expensive ingredients, such as chicken and ham, prawns and shrimps, even a piece of well-flavoured cheese. The croquettes are a standby of Andaluz housewives. Pasties and pies are more frequently to be found in the northern provinces of Spain, particularly Galicia.

The Gallegos, inhabitants of the rocky northern coast, share something of a common culinary heritage with the other Gaelic speaking nations of Europe, including the Welsh and the Scots. Baking comes naturally to these northerners. Spanish pastry doughs are not designed to be crisp – they are more like a pizza dough than a pie-crust, although there is no reason why you shouldn't use your own favourite shortcrust or puff pastry. Spain does have a repertoire of fat-shortened pastries, both short and puff. But they are normally used for sweet biscuits, such as the shortbread-like *mantecados* and the dusty cinnamon-flavoured *polverones* of Christmas.

Andalucían cooks, experts in the art of frying, learn at their mothers' elbows to make the basic white sauce, a panada, for croquettes. Along with the tortilla (page 66), croquettes are a basic of Andaluz culinary tradition. Cheap and delicious, sometimes made only with a good strong broth from a boiled chicken or a ham-flavoured stock, croquettes are a standard of the tapa menu. Careful housewives dry leftover bread for breadcrumbs for the coating, and freshly-made breadcrumbs can be bought in any village bakery.

Croquettes are always served piping hot from the frying pan (skillet). They freeze well and, if they are small, can be fried straight from the freezer. Pies are served hot or cold as a quick snack at any time of the day.

Shrimp croquettes
Croquetas de gambas

Shrimps are the classic filling for *croquetas* in the sea-front bars and *chozos* of Andalucía. If you can get fresh shrimps, use the broth in which you cook them to make the sauce.

Makes 20–25 croquettes   Serves 4 as a starter

THE FILLING
5 tablespoons olive oil or 125 g (4 oz) (½ cup) butter
4 rounded tablespoons plain (all-purpose) flour
1 small glass of sherry
450 ml (¾ pint) (2 cups) fish broth or milk
125 g (4 oz) peeled shrimps, chopped
1 tablespoon chopped parsley

1 teaspoon paprika
salt and pepper

THE COATING
3 tablespoons seasoned plain (all-purpose) flour
1 egg, beaten with 2 tablespoons milk
4–5 tablespoons toasted breadcrumbs
oil for frying

Heat the oil or butter in a saucepan. Stir in the flour and let it froth up for a moment. Stir in the sherry. Beat in the rest of the liquid gradually with a wooden spoon. Cook over a gentle heat until you have a very thick soft sauce. Stir in the chopped shrimps and parsley. Taste and add the paprika and salt and pepper.

Spread the mixture on a plate and cover it with another inverted plate. Leave to cool and firm in the fridge for an hour or two – overnight if possible.

When you are ready to cook, spread the flour on one plate, the egg-and-milk on a second, and the breadcrumbs on a third.

With a knife, cut the filling into 20–25 short stubby fingers. Roll each finger first in the flour, and then in the egg mixture, and finally press it firmly into the breadcrumbs. Continue until the filling is all used up.

Heat 2 fingers' depth (3 cm/1 inch) of oil in a frying pan (skillet). When it is lightly hazed with blue, add the croquettes a few at a time – not too many or the oil temperature will drop. Fry them crisp and golden brown.

Serve the croquettes piping hot from the pan.

Chicken croquettes
Croquetas de pollo

Spanish boiling fowls are small and well-flavoured but tough. They are jointed and simmered with pulses and fresh vegetables and often served like the French *pot-au-feu*: first a bowl of strong broth, followed by the meat and vegetables as a second course. Leftovers from the Sunday boiled chicken – *puchero* – go to make *croquetas* for Monday. Make double quantities for the freezer.

Makes 20–25 croquettes   Serves 3–4 as a starter

THE FILLING
5 tablespoons olive oil or 125 g (4 oz) (½ cup) butter
4 rounded tablespoons plain (all-purpose) flour
450 ml (¾ pint) (2 cups) chicken broth or milk
125 g (4 oz) cooked chicken breast, chopped finely
1 tablespoon chopped parsley
½ teaspoon grated nutmeg
salt and pepper

THE COATING
3–4 tablespoons seasoned plain (all-purpose) flour
1 egg, beaten with 2 tablespoons milk
4–5 tablespoons toasted breadcrumbs
oil for frying

Heat the oil or butter in a saucepan. Stir in the flour and let it froth up for a moment. Beat in the liquid gradually with a wooden spoon. Cook over a gentle heat until you have a very thick soft sauce – the more skilful you become, the thinner you can make the sauce, and the more delicate the croquettes will be.

Stir in the chopped chicken, parsley and nutmeg. Taste and add salt and pepper. Spread the mixture on a plate and cover it with another inverted plate. Leave to cool and firm in the fridge for an hour or two – overnight if possible.

When you are ready to cook, spread the seasoned flour on one plate, the egg-and-milk on a second, and the breadcrumbs on a third.

With a knife, mark the chicken sauce into 20–25 short stubby fingers. Roll each finger first in the flour, and then in the egg mixture, and finally press it firmly into the breadcrumbs. All surfaces should be well coated or the croquette will burst in the hot oil. Continue until the sauce is all used up.

Heat two fingers' depth (3 cm/1 inch) of oil in a frying pan (skillet). When it is lightly hazed with blue, slip in the croquettes a few at a time – not too many or the oil temperature will drop. Fry them crisp and golden brown. Serve the croquettes piping hot from the pan.

> *Spanish housewives make up their own broth with vegetables and leftover bones. This gives added flavour and aroma to many dishes.*
> *To make your own stock, boil a chicken carcass or 500g (1 lb) fish bones and heads in 600ml (1 pint) (2½ cups) water, with an onion, carrot, celery stick, bay leaf, a few black peppercorns and a little salt. Strain and use as required.*

Tuna croquettes
Croquetas de atún

This particular recipe comes from a small bar-restaurant outside La Linea. The vine-covered terrace overlooks the Bay of Gibraltar, which perhaps explains the inclusion of that most British of seasonings, Worcestershire sauce. Make extra for freezing.

Makes 20–25 croquettes   Serves 4 as a starter

THE FILLING
a 198g (7 oz) can of tuna in oil or brine
5 tablespoons olive oil or 125g (4 oz) (½ cup) butter
4 rounded tablespoons plain (all-purpose) flour
450 ml (¾ pint) (2 cups) fish broth or milk
1 tablespoon chopped parsley
1 teaspoon paprika
¼ teaspoon Worcestershire sauce
salt and pepper

THE COATING
3 tablespoons seasoned plain (all-purpose) flour
1 egg, beaten with 2 tablespoons milk
4–5 tablespoons toasted breadcrumbs
oil for frying

Drain the tuna and flake it.
    Heat the oil or butter in a saucepan. Stir in the flour and let it froth up for a moment. Beat in the liquid gradually with a wooden spoon. Cook over a gentle heat until you have a very thick soft sauce (the thinner you can make the sauce, the more delicate the croquettes will be).

Stir in the flaked tuna, parsley, paprika and Worcestershire sauce. Taste and add salt and pepper. Spread the mixture on a plate and cover it with an inverted plate. Leave to cool and firm in the fridge for an hour or two – overnight if possible.

When you are ready to cook, spread the flour on one plate, the egg-and-milk on a second, and the breadcrumbs on a third.

With a knife, mark the chicken sauce into 20–25 short stubby fingers. Roll each finger first in the flour, and then in the egg mixture, and finally press it firmly into the breadcrumbs. Continue until the sauce it all used up.

Heat 2 fingers' depth (3 cm/1 inch) of oil in a frying pan (skillet). When it is lightly hazed with smoke, add the croquettes – not too many at once or the oil temperature will drop. Fry them until crisp and golden.

Serve the croquettes piping hot.

Cheese croquettes
Croquetas de queso

Spain has a large repertoire of matured hard cheeses of which the best-known is Manchego, a ewe's milk cheese from the central plateau of La Mancha. The little fine-flavoured pieces from near the rind go into this economical but delicious treat. Make a batch for the freezer – they de-frost in a moment.

Makes 20–25 croquettes   Serves 3–4 as a starter

THE FILLING
5 tablespoons olive oil or 125 g (4 oz) (½ cup) butter
4 rounded tablespoons plain (all-purpose) flour
1 wine glass of sherry
300 ml (½ pint) (1¼ cups) chicken broth or milk
4 tablespoons grated strong cheese (Manchego, Cheddar or Gruyère)
1 tablespoon grated onion (optional)

salt and pepper

THE COATING
3–4 tablespoons seasoned plain (all-purpose) flour
1 egg, beaten with 2 tablespoons milk
4–5 tablespoons toasted breadcrumbs
oil for frying

TO SERVE
fresh tomato sauce (page 101)

Heat the oil or butter in a saucepan. Stir in the flour and let it froth up for a moment. Beat in the sherry and the rest of the liquid gradually with a wooden spoon. Stir in the grated cheese. Cook over a gentle heat until you have a very thick soft sauce. Add the onion, if used. Taste and add salt and pepper.

Spread the mixture on a plate and cover it with another inverted plate. Leave to cool and firm in the fridge for an hour or two – overnight if possible.

When you are ready to cook, spread the flour on one plate, the egg-and-milk on a second, and the breadcrumbs on a third.

With a knife, mark the filling into 20–25 short stubby fingers. Roll each finger first in the flour, and then in the egg mixture, and finally press it firmly into the breadcrumbs. Make sure each croquette is thoroughly coated. Continue until the filling is all used up.

Heat 2 fingers' depth (3 cm/1 inch) of oil in a frying pan (skillet). When it is lightly hazed, add the croquettes a few at a time – not too many or the oil temperature will drop. Fry them crisp and golden.

Serve the croquettes hot and juicy, with fresh tomato sauce for dipping.

Spanish housewives make their own breadcrumbs to use in many dishes. Make your own with stale bread, sliced and dried in a very low oven until it is crisp and pale gold. Crush in a food processor, or wrap the crisped bread in a clean towel and run a rolling pin over it until it is thoroughly crumbled. Store in an airtight tin and use as required.

Ham croquettes
Croquetas de jamón

These are usually made with the well-flavoured scrag-ends of the salt-cured mountain ham, jamón serrano, which is the most valuable flavouring ingredient in the Spanish kitchen. The liquor for the basic sauce is often the broth made with a ham bone – nothing is wasted in the Spanish kitchen. Make extra for freezing.

Makes 20–25 croquettes   Serves 3–4 as a starter

THE FILLING
5 tablespoons olive oil or
    125 g (4 oz) (½ cup)
    butter
4 rounded tablespoons
    plain (all-purpose) flour
100 g (3½ oz) (½ cup)
    finely chopped ham
    (jamón serrano or
    cooked ham)
450 ml (¾ pint) (2 cups)
    ham or chicken broth, or
    milk
1 hard-boiled egg, chopped
    finely (optional)

2 tablespoons chopped
    parsley
salt and pepper

THE COATING
3–4 tablespoons seasoned
    plain (all-purpose) flour
1 egg, beaten with 2
    tablespoons milk
4–5 tablespoons toasted
    breadcrumbs
oil for frying

Heat the oil or butter in a saucepan. Stir in the flour and let it
fry for a moment without taking colour. Add the chopped
ham. Beat in the liquid gradually with a wooden spoon.
Cook over a gentle heat until you have a very thick soft
sauce.

Stir in the chopped egg, if used, and the parsley. Taste and
add salt and pepper. Spread the mixture on a plate and cover
it with another inverted plate. Leave to cool and firm in the
fridge for an hour or two – overnight if possible.

When you are ready to cook, spread the flour on one
plate, the egg-and-milk on a second, and the breadcrumbs
on a third.

With a knife, mark the filling into 20–25 short stubby
fingers. Roll each finger first in the flour, and then in the egg
mixture, and finally press it firmly into the breadcrumbs.
Check that all surfaces are well coated. Continue until the
sauce is all used up.

Heat 2 fingers' depth (3 cm/1 inch) of oil in a frying pan
(skillet). When it is lightly hazed with smoke, slip in the
croquettes – not too many at once or the oil temperature
will drop. Fry them until crisp.

Serve the croquettes hot from the pan.

---

*Domecq founder Pedro Domecq came to a most unfortunate
end. As a cure from rheumatism, he was suspended over a
tub of boiling water. One dreadful day, the supports to
Pedro's chair snapped and he was plunged into the
cauldron.*

Mushroom croquettes
Croquetas de setas

I have had these made with saffron milk caps in Valencia and wild field mushrooms in Andalucía. They were most delicious of all made with finely grated truffles in Morella, which is a beautiful fortified village in Castellón. The inhabitants of this village have only recently discovered the commercial value of the black diamonds found under the scrub oaks which clothe their rocky mountain slopes. Cultivated mushrooms will do just as well in this recipe, unless you have an expert eye for spotting edible wild fungi. These croquettes freeze perfectly.

Makes 20–25 croquettes   Serves 3–4 as a starter   (Pictured on page 89)

THE FILLING
5 tablespoons olive oil or
   150g (5oz) (½ cup)
   butter
125g (4oz) mushrooms,
   chopped finely
125g (4oz) (1 cup) plain
   (all-purpose) flour
1 wine glass of dry sherry
300ml (½ pint) (1¼ cups)
   chicken broth or milk
2 tablespoons chopped
   parsley

salt and pepper

THE COATING
3–4 tablespoons seasoned
   plain (all-purpose) flour
1 egg, beaten with 2
   tablespoons milk
4–5 tablespoons toasted
   breadcrumbs
oil for frying

Heat the oil or butter in a saucepan. Sauté the mushrooms briefly. Stir in the flour and fry it for a moment. Add the sherry and beat in the rest of the liquid gradually with a wooden spoon. Cook over a gentle heat until you have a very thick soft sauce. Stir in the parsley. Check the seasoning and add salt and pepper.

Spread the mixture on a plate and cover it with another inverted plate. Leave to cool and firm in the fridge for an hour or two – overnight if possible.

When you are ready to cook, spread the flour on one plate, the egg-and-milk on a second, and the breadcrumbs on a third.

With a knife, mark the mushroom mixture into 20–25 short stubby fingers. Roll each finger first in the flour, and then in the egg mixture, and finally press it firmly into the breadcrumbs. Make sure all surfaces are well coated.

Continue until the filling is all used up.

Heat 2 fingers' depth (3 cm/1 inch) of oil in a frying pan (skillet). When it is smoking hot, slip in the croquettes – a few at a time or the oil temperature will drop. Fry them until golden brown.

Serve the croquettes as they come out of the pan.

Spiced meat pasties
Empanadillas de Orense

The spicy meat filling for these pasties is typically Gallician. To wrap it, I give one of the simplest of Spanish pastry doughs. Sometimes these doughs are raised with yeast, like a bread dough – this warm water crust is more like those used for English pork pies. The recipe can be adapted to make one large flat pie for cutting – it will need longer baking at a slightly lower temperature – follow the instructions on page 146.

Makes 25–30 bite-sized pasties   *Serves 5–6 as a starter*

THE FILLING
2 tablespoons olive oil
1 onion, chopped
1 garlic clove, crushed
2 red sweet peppers, hulled, de-seeded and chopped
50 g (2 oz) salt-cured ham or lean bacon, diced
50 g (2 oz) chorizo, or salami plus 1 teaspoon paprika, diced
250 g (8 oz) meat, cubed small (pork, lamb or veal)
1 wine glass of white wine or sherry

3–4 saffron threads, soaked in 1 tablespoon boiling water
1 teaspoon thyme
salt and pepper

THE OIL PASTRY
300 g (10 oz) (2½ cups) self-raising flour, plus extra for rolling
½ teaspoon salt
4 tablespoons olive oil, plus extra for greasing
2 tablespoons white wine
150 ml (¼ pint) (⅔ cup) milk or water

Heat the oil in a frying pan (skillet) and gently fry the onion, garlic and peppers. When the vegetables are soft, push them to one side and add the ham or bacon and chorizo or salami and fry that. Add the paprika if using the salami. Add the meat. Sauté it until it takes a little colour. Splash in the wine or sherry, and add the saffron with its water and the thyme.

Bubble up, lid and simmer until the liquid has evaporated and the meat is tender. Taste and add salt and pepper. Leave aside to cool while you make the pastry.

Preheat the oven to Gas Mark 6/200°C/400°F.

To make the pastry, make a well in the flour and sprinkle in the salt. Put the oil, wine and milk or water into a small pan and heat it to blood temperature. Pour the warm liquid into the flour, and work the dry and wet ingredients together until you have a soft elastic dough. Work it some more until it is smooth and elastic.

Roll out the pastry thinly on a well-floured board with a floured rolling pin. Cut it into rounds with a sharp-edged wine glass. Put a teaspoon of the filling into the centre of each disc. Wet the edges and fold one half over the other to enclose the filling. Mark the edges with a fork to seal. Transfer the pasties to an oiled baking sheet.

Bake in the oven for 10–15 minutes, until the pastry is golden brown. Serve hot or cold.

Note: if you prefer, you can deep-fry the pasties as for the croquettes – in which case, they are nicest hot.

Spiced mincemeat pasties
Empanadillas de picadillo

These were one of my favourites when I was a young teenager in Madrid. My mother's Spanish cook used to make them for parties, and I would have a plateful of them for my supper as a reward for helping her.

Makes 25–30 bite-sized pasties   Serves 5–6 as a starter   (Pictured on page 107)

2 tablespoons olive oil, plus extra for greasing
1 garlic clove, chopped
½ onion, chopped finely
250 g (8 oz) minced (ground) meat
1 teaspoon plain (all-purpose) flour, plus extra for rolling
1 tablespoon raisins, soaked in a small glass of sherry
1 tablespoon pine kernels or flaked almonds
½ teaspoon ground cloves
1 teaspoon ground cinnamon
500 g (1 lb) pastry (short, puff, bread dough, or Spanish on page 140)
salt and pepper

Heat the oil in a small frying pan (skillet). Fry the garlic and onion for a few moments; then add the meat. Turn it until it changes colour and the moisture evaporates. Stir in the flour and fry it for a moment. Add the raisins with their sherry. Allow all to bubble up to evaporate the alcohol and thicken the sauce (you may need a splash of water too). Stir in the nuts and the spices. Taste and add salt and pepper. Leave aside to cool.

Preheat the oven to Gas Mark 6/200°C/400°F.

Roll out the pastry thinly on a well-floured board, and cut it into rounds with a sharp-edged wine glass. Drop teaspoons of the savoury meat into the middle of each round. Dampen the edges of the pastry and fold one half over the other to enclose the filling. Press the edges together with a fork.

Arrange the pasties on a well-greased baking sheet. Bake in the oven for 10–15 minutes, until the pastry is well gilded.

Note: if you prefer, fry the pasties in shallow oil, turning them once.

Fresh sausages with home-made tomato sauce (page 25)
French fries (page 56)
Fried quail's eggs (page 75)
Ham and cheese fritters (page 148)
Cherry tomatoes mimosa (page 34)
Breadcrumbed chicken (page 122)

Gallician pork pie (page 146)
Spiced oxtail stew (page 116)
Gratin of chard stalks (page 55)
Meatballs in tomato sauce (page 101)
Frittered prawns (page 149)

Tuna and tomato pasties
Empanadillas de Valencia

The inshore fleet of the Mediterranean coast used to fish the giant tuna which, until stocks were depleted in recent years, migrated in huge shoals through its waters. Canned tuna fish remains a storecupboard staple of the Spanish kitchen. This simple recipe is popular in the tapa bars of Valencia.

Makes 25–30 bite-sized pasties   Serves 5–6 as a starter

a 198 g (7 oz) can of tuna
1 tablespoon olive oil, plus extra for greasing
1 garlic clove, chopped finely
1 tablespoon chopped onion
500 g (1 lb) tomatoes, skinned and chopped (fresh or canned)
1 teaspoon thyme
1 teaspoon chopped parsley
500 g (1 lb) pastry (short, puff, bread dough, or Spanish on page 140)
flour for rolling
salt and pepper

Drain and flake the tuna.

Heat the oil in a frying pan (skillet) and turn the garlic and onion in it until they take colour. Add the tomatoes and thyme and cook over a high heat so that the tomatoes melt into a thick rich sauce. Stir in the tuna and the parsley. Leave aside to cool.

Preheat the oven to Gas Mark 6/200°C/400°F.

Roll out the pastry thinly on a well-floured board, and cut it into rounds with a sharp-edged wine glass. Drop teaspoons of the cold tuna and tomato into the middle of each round. Dampen the edges of the pastry and fold one half over the other to enclose the filling. Press the edges together with a fork.

Arrange the pasties on a well-greased baking sheet. Bake in the oven for 10–15 minutes, until the pastry is well gilded.

Note: if you like, fry the pasties in oil instead, turning them once.

Gallician pork pie
Empanada de lomo

This is Galicia's most traditional pie. Make individual pasties (*empanadillas*), following the instructions on page 140, or, as here, a juicy pie (*empanada*) for cutting. Either way it's lovely picnic food, as well as a delicious tapa.

Makes 18–20 tapa portions   Serves 4 as a starter   (Pictured on page 144)

500 g (1 lb) lean pork, cubed small
2 wine glasses of white wine
½ teaspoon thyme
1 teaspoon marjoram
1 teaspoon paprika
½ teaspoon pepper
1 onion, chopped
1 garlic clove, chopped
1 green pepper, hulled, de-seeded and chopped

3 tablespoons olive oil, plus extra for greasing
½ teaspoon salt
250 g (8 oz) peeled, diced potato
500 g (1 lb) pastry (short, puff, bread dough, or Spanish on page 140)
flour for rolling

Put the pork to marinate overnight in the wine, herbs, paprika and pepper.

Drain the meat, reserving the marinade.

Fry the onion, garlic and green pepper in the olive oil until they take a little colour. Push the vegetables to one side. Add the meat and turn it in the hot oil until it begins to fry. Sprinkle in the salt. Pour in the marinade, bubble up, turn down the heat, and cover. Leave to simmer for 20–25 minutes until the meat is tender. Add the potato cubes and simmer until the potato is tender. Remove the lid and bubble up until the juices have nearly all evaporated. Taste and adjust the seasoning. Leave aside to cool.

Preheat the oven to Gas Mark 5/190°C/375°F.

Divide the pastry in half and roll out each piece on a well-floured board into a 25 cm (10-inch) square. Transfer one sheet to a greased baking tray and spread on the filling, leaving a 2 finger width (3 cm/1 inch) margin all round. Dampen the edges of the pastry and lay the second sheet on top. Press the edges together, wet the top edge, and turn it over in a scallop shape to seal. Prick the top with a fork.

Bake in the oven for 25–30 minutes, until the pastry is well gilded. Serve hot or cold, cut into squares.

Spinach pasties
Empanadillas de espinacas

Pasties can be made with a variety of vegetables. Swiss chard stalks and leaves, sliced leeks with cabbage, puréed aubergine (eggplant), or mashed potatoes mixed with onion and parsley. The cheese in the mixture adds protein and flavour, the egg binds it.

Makes 25–30 bite-sized pasties   Serves 6 as a starter

375 g (12 oz) cooked
  spinach (fresh or frozen)
2 tablespoons olive oil,
  plus extra for greasing
1 garlic clove, crushed
2 tablespoons dry sherry
½ teaspoon grated nutmeg
juice of ½ lemon
50 g (2 oz) (⅔ cup) grated
  strong cheese
  (Manchego, Cheddar or
  parmesan)

1 egg, beaten lightly
500 g (1 lb) pastry (short,
  puff, bread dough, or
  Spanish on page 140)
flour for rolling
salt and pepper

Preheat the oven to Gas Mark 6/200°C/400°F.

Mix together the spinach, oil, garlic, sherry, nutmeg, lemon juice, cheese and egg. Add salt and pepper to taste.

Roll out the pastry thinly on a well-floured board, and cut into rounds with a sharp-edged wine glass. Put teaspoonfuls of the savoury spinach mixture into the middle of each round. Dampen the edges of the pastry and fold one half over the other to enclose the filling. Press the edges together with a fork.

Arrange the pasties on a well-greased baking sheet. Bake in the oven for 10–15 minutes, until the pastry is well gilded.

Note: if you prefer, fry the pasties in shallow oil, turning them once.

The great Domecq sherry dynasty, founded by Pedro Domecq, dates back to 1730. Within five years the company had a Royal Warrant from King Fernando VII.

Cheese fritters
Buñuelos de queso

These crisp little morsels must be enjoyed hot from the frying pan (skillet). They are so simple a child can make them, and they are perfect for a light summer lunch.

Makes 15–20 fritters   Serves 3–4 as a starter

3 eggs
3 tablespoons milk
175 g (6 oz) (1½ cups) grated hard cheese (Manchego, Cheddar or Gruyère)
3 tablespoons plain (all-purpose) flour
1 tablespoon chopped parsley

1 tablespoon grated onion
1 teaspoon paprika
oil for frying
salt and pepper
fresh tomato sauce (page 101), spiked with ¼ teaspoon cayenne pepper, to serve

Beat the eggs and milk lightly together. Stir in the cheese. Work in the flour, beating to avoid lumps. Add the parsley, onion and paprika. Season with salt and pepper.

Heat 2 fingers' depth (3 cm/1 inch) of oil in a frying pan (skillet). When it is lightly hazed with blue, drop in teaspoons of the mixture – not too many at once or the oil temperature will drop. Fry them crisp and golden brown, turning once.

Serve piping hot, with chilli and tomato sauce for dipping.

Ham and cheese fritters
Delicias de jamón y queso

A dish for those in a hurry, this is a combination of *pain perdu* and *croque monsieur* – lovely and crisp and delicious.

Makes 8 small sandwiches   Serves 2 as a light meal   (Pictured on page 143)

4 slices of bread
2 slices of ham (jamón serrano, if possible)
2 slices of hard cheese (Manchego or Cheddar)

1 egg
2 tablespoons milk
4 tablespoons olive oil
salt and pepper

Make sandwiches with the bread, ham and cheese, and cut them neatly into quarters. Beat the egg with the milk and season it with salt and pepper.

Dip the sandwiches in the egg mixture. Fry them in the oil, turning once, until golden brown on both sides.

Serve piping hot, spiked with cocktail sticks.

Frittered prawns
Gambas en gabadina

This recipe makes the most of luxuriously expensive deep-water prawns. If you manage to find raw ones, use the cooking water to replace the plain water.

Makes 12 tapa portions   Serves 4 as a starter   (Pictured on page 144)

12 large cooked prawns
600 ml (1 pint) (2½ cups) water
1 small glass of dry sherry
a bouquet garni (1 bay leaf, a sprig of thyme and a sprig of parsley)
½ onion
4 tablespoons olive oil or 75 g (3 oz) (⅓ cup) butter
75 g (3 oz) (¾ cup) plain (all-purpose) flour
salt and pepper

THE COATING
3 tablespoons seasoned plain (all-purpose) flour
1 egg, beaten with 2 tablespoons milk
4–5 tablespoons toasted breadcrumbs
oil for frying

TO SERVE
quartered lemons and garlic mayonnaise (page 104)

Peel the prawns, leaving the tails on. Put the peelings, heads and all, in a saucepan with the water, sherry, bouquet garni and onion. Bring to the boil, turn the heat down and simmer for 20–30 minutes. Strain, pressing down to extract all the juices. Return the stock to the pan and simmer until you have 450 ml (¾ pint) (2 cups) of well-flavoured broth. Taste and add salt and pepper.

Heat the oil or butter in a saucepan. Stir in the flour and let it froth up for a moment. Beat in the prawn stock gradually with a wooden spoon. Cook over a gentle heat until you have a thick coating sauce.

Dip the prawns in the sauce and coat them all over, leaving just the tails exposed. Then leave them to cool and firm in the fridge for an hour or two.

Spread the flour on one plate, the egg-and-milk on a second, and the breadcrumbs on a third.

Dip each coated prawn first in the flour, and then in the egg mixture, and finally press it firmly into the breadcrumbs.

Heat 2 fingers' depth (3 cm/1 inch) of oil in a frying pan (skillet). When it is lightly hazed with blue, slip in the prawns a few at a time. Fry them until crisp and brown.

Serve the prawns hot from the pan, with quartered lemons and garlicky mayonnaise for dipping.

Salt cod fritters
Buñuelos de bacalao

Salt cod was the fasting food of Mediterranean Europe during the Middle Ages. The coastal fishermen of the Atlantic seaboard used their harvest of salted cod both as a trade item and for food on their long sea journeys. The Scandinavians traded theirs for the wine and oil of the warm south – a commercial exchange of great economic importance. Canned tuna and a few anchovies can substitute for the *bacalao* if it is hard to find.

Makes 20–24 fritters   Serves 4–5 as a starter

250 g (8 oz) salt cod (bacalao), soaked for 48 hours to de-salt
500 g (1 lb) (5⅓ cups) mashed potatoes
2 eggs
125 g (4 oz) (1 cup) self-raising flour
1 garlic clove, crushed
1 tablespoon grated onion
1 tablespoon chopped parsley
½ teaspoon grated nutmeg
oil for frying
salt and pepper
fresh tomato sauce (page 101), to serve

With your fingers, skin and remove any bones from the salt cod. Flake it small. Beat the fish into the potatoes and work in the eggs and flour. Stir in the garlic, onion, parsley and nutmeg and a little pepper. Taste and add salt if necessary.

Heat 2 fingers' depth (3 cm/1 inch) of oil in a deep frying pan (skillet). When it is lightly hazed with blue, drop in teaspoons of the mixture. Turn them when they are puffed up and crisp. Drain on kitchen paper.

Serve piping hot, with tomato sauce for dipping.

Choosing your tapas

Back in Britain, I and my family continue to enjoy the Spanish way with tapas, but adapted to our needs here. There are many dishes which require a minimum of preparation and cooking, or can be prepared ahead, and some which freeze well – and, since the portions are always small and individual, they can be unfrozen fast. Tapas are perfect for parties – a trouble-free way of providing for an expandable number of guests. Or simply to add entertainment to an ordinary meal shared with a friend. A dish or two of something which needs no cooking – marinated olives, a slice of cured ham or sausage, a bit of potato salad – staves off the pangs of hunger until you have prepared something hot and delicious. And if more people arrive meanwhile, well, more bread and another small dish can be put out, and maybe a tortilla or a plate of hot french fries added to the menu. When it's all on the table, the cook can sit down and pick and share with the guests.

When serving tapas as a party meal, a fair rule of thumb is to make as many main dishes as you have guests. Either set out most of the dishes at the same time, buffet-style, bringing in a hot one or two later. Or organise the meal into the familiar two courses, starting with the little basic tapas of olives, nuts, cheese and ham, plus salads and cold dishes. By the time you bring in the main dishes, your guests will have accustomed themselves to this delightful informal eating, and will happily organise their own platefuls. Provide plenty of good bread for people to mop up sauces and wipe fingers.

Cold dry sherry – of course this must be La Ina – is the perfect accompaniment to a tapa meal, with perhaps a move to a good Spanish red or white wine, like Domecq's Riojan wine, to follow. Have water and extra glasses on the table too. Wine-producing nations customarily drink wine and water alternately.

A winter tapa party

Here's some lovely warming spicy food, mostly from the high central plateau of Spain, where the winters are cold. The oxtail stew is delicious on a winter night. It can be prepared well ahead, as can everything but the shrimp fritters.

Serves 6–8 (*A selection is pictured on page 144*)

Olives (page 14)
Spiced peanuts (page 16)
Cabrales, Roquefort or Stilton cheese (page 20)
Rice salad with tuna fish (page 41)
Black pudding (page 23)

Baked potatoes with oil and onion (page 47)
Gratin of cardoons or chard stalks (page 55)
Spiced oxtail stew (page 116)
Gallician pork pie (page 146)
Meatballs in tomato sauce (page 101)
Shrimp fritters (page 96)

A spring tapa party

Spring offers a lovely opportunity to serve young vegetables. Look for scarlet radishes, baby courgettes (zucchini) and carrots, early asparagus and peppers, and young broad and green beans, to serve raw. Wash the vegetables carefully, and present them complete with any leaves flanked by a dish of coarse salt, quartered lemons and a flagon of first-pressing virgin olive oil so that guests can dip or dress their own as they please.

Serves 6–8 (*A selection is pictured on page 125*)

Olives (page 14)
Raw young vegetables with lemon, oil and salt
Mahon or mature Cheshire cheese (page 19)
Cod's roe salad (page 34)
Spinach or chard leaves dressed with vinegar (page 59)

New potatoes with garlic and saffron (page 56)
Shrimp fritters (page 96)
Crayfish with green sauce (page 95)
Fisherman's mussels (page 93)
Grilled (broiled) spiced hamburgers (page 102)
Griddled marinated lamb's kidneys (page 113)

A summer tapa party

As with the spring tapa party, look for fresh young vegetables to serve raw with good oil, lemon quarters and coarse salt. Chicken or rabbit with garlic is my favourite summer dish – for a delicious al fresco lunch, take the raw ingredients outside and cook it on the barbecue or a little fire.

Serves 6–8   (*A selection is pictured on page 53*)

Olives (page 14)
Raw salad vegetables with lemon, oil and salt
Manchego or well-matured Cheddar cheese (page 19)
Fried baby artichokes (page 50)
Russian salad with mayonnaise (page 31)

Green beans with spiced almonds (page 60)
Chicken with garlic (page 121)
Clams in sherry (page 91)
Steaks with blue cheese (page 102)
Grilled (broiled) prawns (page 88)
Moorish kebabs (page 114)

An autumn tapa party

Almonds and smoked cheese, mushrooms and quail spell the pleasures of autumn. In September the grapes are harvested round Jerez, ready for the labour of love which converts the raw juice into the clear dry aromatic wines which go so well with these dishes.

Serves 6–8   (*A selection is pictured on page 107*)

Olives (page 14)
Salted almonds (page 15)
Smoked Idiazábal or any smoked cheese (page 19)
Spicy chorizo or salami (page 22)
Rice salad with pine kernels (page 40)

Whole broad bean casserole (page 64)
Basque crab (page 98)
Spiced mincemeat pasties (page 142)
Mushroom croquettes (page 139)
Deep-fried spatchcocked quails (page 123)
Grilled (broiled) lamb cutlets with garlic mayonnaise
    (page 104)

A children's tapa party

Children are the most demanding audience a cook ever has to face. They will usually eat only those things which are familiar to them, and are deeply conservative when confronted with the new. I always make plenty of big fat french fries – for which most children have an insatiable appetite. Otherwise, all these recipes are easily recognisable for what they are.

Serves 6–8   (*A selection is pictured on page 143*)

Toasted hazelnuts (page 16)
Cantabria or mild Cheddar cheese (page 20)
Potato crisps (page 26)
Pork scratchings (page 25)
Cherry tomatoes mimosa (page 34)

Fried quail's eggs (page 75)
Ham and cheese fritters (page 148)
Breadcrumbed chicken (page 122)
French fries (page 56)
Fresh sausages (page 25)

A vegetarian tapa party

Spain likes its fish and meat, and rarely has a meal which does not include one or the other, even if it's only a ham bone for flavouring. Careful selection, however, can produce a delicious vegetarian meal – there are also plenty of recipes which can be turned vegetarian by judiciously omitting the ham or bacon which flavours them.

Serves 6–8   (*A selection is pictured on page 54*)

Olives (page 14)
Hot bread with olive oil and garlic (page 26)
New potato salad (page 40)
Artichokes in oil (page 39)

Mixed vegetable omelette (page 78)
Spinach pasties (page 147)
Cheese fritters (page 148)
Courgettes (zucchini) in tomato sauce (page 62)
Aubergine (eggplant) purée (page 48)
Baked mushrooms with parsley and garlic (page 48)

Slimmers' tapas

Spanish cooks are increasingly health-conscious, but do not naturally regard good food with a view to its potential for slimmers. Here is a meal which avoids the obvious high-calorie foods and uses the grill rather than the frying pan (skillet).

Serves 4 (*A selection is pictured on page 72*)

Olives (page 14)
Winkles or whelks with spiced vinegar (page 92)
Salad kebabs (page 42)
Tomatoes with garlic and marjoram (page 44)

Seafood salad (page 44)
Monkfish kebabs (page 84)
Grilled (broiled) prawns and shellfish (page 88)
Spiced grilled (broiled) chicken (page 120)

No-cook tapas

An excellent meal can be produced just by opening a few cans and slicing a tomato or two. Make sure all ingredients are the best quality you can afford. The simpler the recipe, the more important the basic materials.

Serves 4 (*A selection is pictured on page 108*)

Olives (page 14)
Jamón serrano or Parma ham (page 20)
Chorizo or salami (page 22)
Roncal, Manchego or mature Cheddar cheese (page 19)

Beetroot salad (page 42)
Tomatoes with anchovies (page 43)
Canned sardines with onion (page 29)
Canapés of conserved tuna (page 27)
Roast pork and crisps (page 112)

> *The traditional Spanish sherry glass is the copita. It is tall, thin and tulip-shaped. Never fill it more than two-thirds full to appreciate the delicate aroma of the wine.*

Tapas for two

Make up your own combinations — here are a few suggestions. Tapas for two is a good opportunity to try recipes requiring luxury ingredients, which might be too expensive in larger quantities.

(A selection is pictured on page 90)

Olives (page 14)
Manchego or any well-matured hard cheese (page 19)
Asparagus with soft-boiled eggs (page 52)
Tomatoes with anchovies (page 43)

Peppery potatoes (page 58)
Grilled (broiled) or plain oysters or grilled (broiled) prawns
   (page 88)
Grilled (broiled) lamb cutlets with garlic mayonnaise
   (page 104)

Tapas for eight or more

When you are dealing with this quantity of people, increase the amounts of two or three of the dishes, rather than adding yet another one to the list. I suggest three deep-fried dishes — once you have the oil hot, it's easy enough to carry on frying. The other dishes to be served hot can be kept in a low oven until you are ready for them.

(A selection is pictured on page 126)

Olives (page 14)
Jamón serrano or Parma ham (page 20)
Spiced peanuts (page 16)
Chicory and blue cheese (page 43)
Potato mayonnaise with red sweet peppers (page 32)

Broad bean omelette or asparagus sprue omelette (page 76
   and 74)
Fried squid (page 92)
Shrimp fritters (page 96)
Aubergine (eggplant) fritters (page 50)
Spiced meat pasties (page 140)
Chicken with red sweet peppers (page 120)
Veal kidneys with sherry (page 112)

Tapas for four

Four is a good number for a tapa party – it gives the opportunity for a little choice. The broad beans and fried vegetables are easily prepared ahead of time. The croquettes can also be made ahead, ready to be deep-fried at the last minute, while you finish the fish steaks and pork medallions under the grill.

(*A selection is pictured on page 71*)

Olives (page 14)
Salted almonds (page 15)
Tomatoes with anchovies (page 43)
Eggs with mayonnaise (page 33)

Broad beans with ham (page 52)
Fried green peppers or fried baby artichokes (page 49 and 50)
Chicken croquettes (page 134)
Griddled tuna or swordfish steaks (page 80)
Pork medallions with lemon and marjoram (page 105)

Tapas for six

All these recipes can be prepared ahead of time. The omelette, peppers and tomatoes are delicious served at room temperature. The prawns need only to be heated in their oil, the kebabs and marinated pork fillet take only a few minutes to finish off under or on the grill.

(*A selection is pictured on page 89*)

Olives (page 14)
Manchego or mature Cheddar cheese (page 19)
Salted almonds (page 15)
Beetroot salad (page 42)
Fresh pickled anchovies (page 37)

Spanish potato omelette (page 66)
Fried peppers (red sweet or green) (page 49)
Tomatoes stuffed with pine kernels (page 60)
Prawns in garlic and oil (page 94)
Chicken kebabs with fresh tomato sauce (page 127)
Marinated griddled pork fillet (page 110)

Index